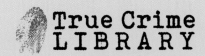
True Crime
LIBRARY

INFAMOUS
TERRORISTS

DRUG CARTELS AND SMUGGLERS
INFAMOUS TERRORISTS
ORGANIZED CRIME
MASS MURDERERS
MODERN-DAY PIRATES
SERIAL KILLERS

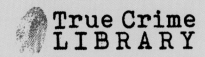
True Crime
LIBRARY

INFAMOUS
TERRORISTS

DOROTHY KAVANAUGH

ELDORADO INK

Eldorado Ink
PO Box 100097
Pittsburgh, PA 15233
www.eldoradoink.com

Produced by OTTN Publishing, Stockton, New Jersey

CPSIA compliance information: Batch#CS2013-2. For further information, contact Eldorado Ink at info@eldoradoink.com.

First printing

1 3 5 7 9 8 6 4 2

Library of Congress Cataloging-in-Publication Data
available from the Library of Congress

ISBN-13: 978-1-61900-031-5 (hc)
ISBN-13: 978-1-61900-032-2 (trade)
ISBN-13: 978-1-61900-033-9 (ebook)

*For information about custom editions, special sales, or premiums,
please contact our special sales department at info@eldoradoink.com.*

TABLE OF CONTENTS

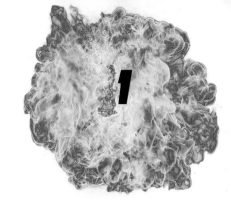

A fire burns in the World Trade Center's north tower on the morning of September 11, 2001, shortly after terrorists crashed an airplane into the building in New York City.

TERRORISM
AN INTRODUCTION

On the morning of September 11, 2001, ten Arab men were among the passengers boarding two commercial jet airplanes at Boston's Logan Airport. Five men got onto each plane secretly carrying utility knives. The two aircraft were bound for Los Angeles, but they never arrived. Instead, once the jets were in the air, the men used their knives to overpower the pilots and crew. They took control of the jets and steered them south toward New York City.

As the airplanes approached New York, the hijackers looked for the city's tallest buildings—the twin towers of the World Trade Center in lower Manhattan. To many people, the towers were a symbol of America's economic strength. At 8:46 A.M., the first of the airplanes flew into the World Trade Center's north tower. It exploded, and burning jet fuel caused an enormous fire.

Some people who were in lower floors were able to evacuate, but hundreds more were trapped inside the building.

Less than 20 minutes later, the second plane struck the south tower. The fires in both buildings caused so much damage that the weakened structures soon collapsed, killing everyone still inside—including firemen, policemen, and emergency workers who had rushed into the buildings trying to save trapped workers.

Those were not the only attacks on the United States that day. Five other secretly armed men had boarded a passenger jet at Washington, D.C.'s Dulles Airport, gained control once it was in the air, and diverted the plane to Arlington, Virginia. At 9:37 A.M. this plane crashed into the Pentagon, the headquarters of the U.S. Department of Defense and a symbol of America's military strength. A fourth airplane was also hijacked that morning; the four men on board planned to fly the plane into either the White House or the U.S. Capitol building. However, when passengers fought back the hijackers crashed the jet into the Pennsylvania countryside.

The September 11 attacks were the deadliest foreign attack on American soil. More than 3,000 people were killed that day. Millions of other Americans were traumatized by the images of the collapsing towers and the charred Pentagon. This, of course, was the purpose of the attacks. The men who had planned the attacks and carried them out were terrorists. They wanted to make Americans afraid, and therefore force the American government to react to the demands of the terrorists and change its policies.

Terrorism involves the use or threat of violence in order to intimidate national governments and force them to change their policies or political direction. This political motivation is what distinguishes the terrorist from, for example, a mass murderer—even though each might commit deadly violence against random civilians.

Those who use terrorism as a method to bring about political change usually target civilians. Bombings, hijackings, and other forms of violence inspire fear and terror in the victims as well as in those who might become victims—thus the term *terrorism*.

Typically, terrorism is a tactic used by a group that has little power against a stronger adversary. In fact, most experts agree that terrorism can only be committed by what the U.S. legal code refers to as "sub-national groups." In other words, the acts of states cannot be said to constitute terrorism—even when those acts represent violence against civilians and are designed to change the policies of another government.

However, states can, and do, sponsor terrorist groups—organizations whose main method of action is terrorism. Countries that are known to have provided financial aid, weapons, and shelter to terrorist groups include Iran, Syria, Cuba, Libya, Sudan, and North Korea. Typically, the United States, Great Britain, and other western states have punished state sponsors of terrorism by imposing economic sanctions, and sometimes by taking military action.

The former dictator of Libya, Muammar Gaddafi, was one of the most notorious sponsors of terrorism. Gaddafi was an Arab nationalist who strongly opposed support of Israel by the United States and other western nations. His government was responsible for financing and planning numerous terrorist attacks during the 1980s. In one April 1986 incident, terrorists set off a bomb at the LaBelle disco in West Berlin, a nightclub that was frequented by American soldiers stationed

DEFINING TERRORISM

Although terrorism is a tactic that has been used for centuries, it is not easy to define. In fact, although the United Nations has been attempting to define the term *terrorism* since 2005, today there remains no international consensus over the meaning of this term.

In trying to develop a definition, some people may refer to the aphorism "one man's terrorist is another man's freedom fighter." By this, they mean that defining certain actions as terrorist may largely depend on the perspective of the definer. For example, a person or group may commit violent acts as part of an armed rebellion against a government. Those who sympathize with or support the rebel group's goals are likely to defend such acts as part of a legitimate attempt to change the existing social order. However, there are critical differences between the "terrorist" and the "freedom fighter," as President Ronald Reagan noted in a 1986 speech:

> "Freedom fighters do not need to terrorize a population into submission. Freedom fighters target the military forces and the organized instruments of repression keeping dictatorial regimes in power. Freedom fighters struggle to liberate their citizens from oppression and to establish a form of government that reflects the will of the people. Now, this is not to say that those who are fighting for freedom are perfect or that we should ignore problems arising from passion and conflict. Nevertheless, one has to be blind, ignorant, or simply unwilling to see the truth if he or she is unable to distinguish between those I just described and terrorists. Terrorists intentionally kill or maim unarmed civilians, often women and children, often third parties who are not in any way part of a dictatorial regime. Terrorists are always the enemies of democracy."

In recent years, several U.S. government agencies have developed their own specific definitions of terrorism. The U.S. Department of Defense defines terrorism as "the calculated use of unlawful violence or threat of unlawful violence to inculcate fear; intended to coerce or to intimidate governments or societies in the pursuit of goals that are generally political, religious, or ideological."

The FBI defines terrorism as "the unlawful use of force and violence against persons or property to intimidate or coerce a government, the civilian population, or any segment thereof, in furtherance of political or social objectives."

The U.S. Department of State defines terrorism to be "premeditated politically motivated violence perpetrated against non-combatant targets by sub-national groups or clandestine agents, usually intended to influence an audience."

in West Germany. Two U.S. soldiers and a woman were killed, and more than 220 others were injured.

The nightclub attack was Gaddafi's retaliation for an incident two weeks earlier, when Libyan jets and warships had engaged a U.S. naval force conducting military exercises in the Gulf of Sidra. This was an area of international waters claimed by Libya. That incident had ended with a Libyan ship damaged and 35 of its sailors killed. The United States responded to the nightclub bombing by launching airstrikes against the Libyan capital, Tripoli, that killed 15 people.

Two years later, terrorists trained and paid by Libya placed a bomb on board a passenger airliner, Pan Am Flight 103, that was flying from London to New York. The bomb exploded about a half

Cuba is among the countries that the United States considers to be state sponsors of terrorism because longtime dictator Fidel Castro often provided aid to rebel groups in Africa and Latin America that carried out terrorist attacks.

hour after takeoff, destroying the plane and killing 259 people. Most of the victims were American or British civilians. Debris from the plane landed in the village of Lockerbie, Scotland, killing 11 more people on the ground.

The United States and the United Kingdom spent three years on a joint investigation of this terrorist attack, eventually concluding that two Libyan intelligence officers had been behind the plot. In 1999, the two men were turned over to western authorities by the Libyan government. One, Abdelbaset al-Megrahi, was convicted and imprisoned in 2001 for his role in the bombing. The other was acquitted. In 2003 the Libyan government also paid millions into a fund to compensate the victims. That same year, Gaddafi renounced the use of terrorism.

Although a non-state organization may be designated as a terrorist group, such organizations often use many tactics aside from terrorism in the pursuit of their goals. Sometimes a terrorist group becomes affiliated with a legal (or illegal) political party. In such cases, the party may have an armed paramilitary wing that uses violence, or the threat of violence, to further the party's goals.

This is the case with Hezbollah, an organization that is active in the Middle Eastern country of Lebanon. Hezbollah has a well-armed military wing that engages in terrorism, with attacks generally aimed at the neighboring state of

Investigators examine the wreckage of Pan Am Flight 103 in a farmer's field near Lockerbie, Scotland, on December 23, 1988. Libya's Muammar Gaddafi financed the bombing.

Israel. However, the organization also provides social programs, such as schools and medical clinics, to Shiite Muslims living in southern Lebanon. Hezbollah also functions as a political party; in 2011 the group won 14 seats in Lebanon's national legislature, and two top figures in Hezbollah hold important positions in the Lebanese government.

Some other terrorist groups that have operated closely with political parties include Umkhonto we Sizwe, a militant wing of the African National Congress (ANC) in South Africa and

the Irish Republican Army (IRA), which was closely associated with the nationalist party Sinn Féin in Northern Ireland. Both of these groups actively employed terrorism from the 1960s until the 1990s, with differing results. By the mid-1990s the ANC's terror campaign, coupled with international pressure, had succeeded in overturning South Africa's system of racial segregation known as apartheid. Since the 1994 election of former Umkhonto we Sizwe commander Nelson Mandela as president of South Africa, the African National Congress has been

Muammar Gaddafi

Nineteen U.S. servicemen were killed in June 1996 when a massive truck bomb destroyed the Khobar Towers apartment complex in Dhahran, Saudi Arabia. A group called Party of God in the Hijaz claimed responsibility for the attack. A U.S. investigation later determined that Iran had probably planned the attack and paid the terrorists who carried it out.

that country's dominant political party.

The goal of the Irish Republican Army, on the other hand, was to drive the British out of Northern Ireland, which had remained part of the United Kingdom after the Republic of Ireland became independent from British rule in the 1920s. Beginning in the late 1960s, the IRA conducted bombings and assassinations; their attacks were often countered by other paramilitary groups that supported the UK government, such as the Ulster Volunteer Force. Three decades of violence mostly ended in 1998, with the signing of the Good Friday accords. The IRA's armed struggle failed to drive the British out of Northern Ireland, which remains part of the United Kingdom. However, today

Sinn Féin is the second-largest political party in Northern Ireland, and participates in the power-sharing government.

Since the late 1990s, world leaders have been very concerned about the rise of international terrorist networks, which conduct attacks in more than one country in order to achieve certain goals. The most infamous of these groups is al-Qaeda, the organization that planned and executed the September 11, 2001, attacks against the United States.

The leaders of al-Qaeda, including the group's founder Osama bin Laden, are Muslims, or followers of the religion known as Islam. They hold some radical beliefs that are not shared by mainstream Muslims. One of these beliefs is that the modern world has become corrupt and degenerate because people no longer properly obey all the teachings of Islam. To change this situation, a goal of al-Qaeda and similar groups is to overthrow the existing governments in Muslim countries in the Middle East and Asia. They want to establish a theocratic government over these lands, called the caliphate, in which all people must obey Islamic laws. Muslims who want to make Islam a central element of government are often referred to as "fundamentalists" or "Islamists."

Although Al-Qaeda is the most widely known terrorist group with an Islamist ideology, it is not the only one. In Indonesia, an organization called Jemaah Islamiyah (JI) has been trying to overthrow the democratic government for more than a decade.

Osama bin Laden

Indonesia is the world's fourth most populous country, and is home to more Muslims than any other nation. The organization's deadliest attack came in 2002, when its terrorists detonated two bombs at a tourist resort on the Indonesian island of Bali, killing more than 200 civilians. Jemaah Islamiyah is also active elsewhere in Asia, as its members have committed attacks in Malaysia, the Philippines, Singapore, and Thailand.

Although in recent years the focus has been on Islamist terrorist groups, it's important to remember that terrorism is a tactic for forcing political change, not an ideology. In the past century terrorism has been employed by adherents of other religions, including Christians, Jews, and Hindus. The tactic has also been used by groups united by national identity (such as Basques, Irish, Kurds, and Palestinians), and by those who follow a certain political theory (Marxism-Leninism or Anarchism, for example).

According to FBI statistics released in 2012, there were more than 10,000 terrorist attacks during the previous year. These attacks affected nearly 45,000 people in 70 countries, with more than 12,500 killed.

The good news is that the frequency of terrorist attacks has been dropping in recent years. The total number of attacks in 2011 was almost 12 percent lower than in 2010, and was 29 percent lower than in 2007. The number of suicide bombings in 2011 (279) had fallen to almost half the number in 2007 (520). However, terrorism continues to be a major concern for governments, and people, all over the world.

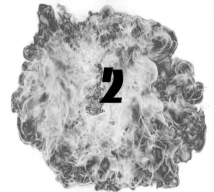

This damage to the Pentagon was caused when al-Qaeda terrorists hijacked American Airlines Flight 77 and crashed it into the building on September 11, 2001. All 59 passengers and crew on the plane were killed, along with the five terrorists and 125 Americans working in the building when it was attacked.

AL-QAEDA
OSAMA BIN LADEN'S DEADLY TERRORIST NETWORK

After the shocking September 11, 2001, attacks on the World Trade Center and the Pentagon, most Americans came to view a shadowy figure named Osama bin Laden as the public face of Islamic terrorism. Bin Laden was not a newcomer to terrorist activities, however. During the 1990s, he and the international terrorist network that he had established, called al-Qaeda, had planned, financed, and carried out numerous attacks against American and western targets. Because many of these attacks had occurred in distant foreign lands, they were relatively easy to overlook for ordinary Americans. It was not until the horrible events of September 11 that many people realized the United States was at war with a determined, fanatical enemy.

Osama bin Laden was born on March 10, 1957, into a wealthy family in Saudi Arabia. His father was a bil-lionaire who owned a construction company. Despite his family's wealth, Osama was raised simply, with his Muslim family carefully observing the teachings of Muhammad ibn Abd al-Wahhab. In the mid-1700s this Muslim cleric had come to believe that Muslims had fallen away from the true faith and preached for a return to the fundamentals of Islam. Wahhabism, the strict form of Sunni Islam that evolved from his teachings, is the mainstream form of the religion in Saudi Arabia today.

Osama bin Laden attended college in Saudi Arabia, where he studied engineering and took business courses. But in December 1979, an event occurred that would change his life forever: the Soviet Union invaded Afghanistan in order to prop up a Communist government in the central Asian country.

Afghan Muslims soon began to fight back against the occupying Soviets, whom they saw as "godless" invaders that would persecute believers. Those who resisted the Soviets became known as *mujahideen*, which means "those waging jihad."

Young Muslims from outside Afghanistan were inspired by the *mujahideen*'s struggle against their well-armed enemy. A few thousand Arabs traveled to Afghanistan to join the resistance. Osama bin Laden was one of them. He used his family's money and connections in the construction business to help buy weapons for the *mujahideen* and to create camps where

they could be trained. His company constructed tunnels and bunkers in the mountains of eastern Afghanistan that the *mujahideen* could use to hide from Soviet counterattacks.

Some of the Afghan *mujahideen* groups also secretly received weapons and funding from the United States. At this time the U.S. and Soviet Union were embroiled in the Cold War, and U.S. leaders believed that supporting the *mujahideen* would weaken the Soviets.

The occupation of Afghanistan did turn out to be a costly and unpopular quagmire for the Soviet Union. Russian

Afghan *mujahideen* return to their village, which has been destroyed by Soviet forces, 1986.

troops finally pulled out in 1989. The Soviet Union itself would only last a few more years, breaking apart in 1992.

By this time, Osama bin Laden had decided that success of the *mujahideen* against the Soviet Union could be duplicated in other countries where Muslims lived. He had come to believe that the influence of modern Western values and culture posed a threat to Islam, and that the worldwide Muslim community (or *umma*) had strayed from the true path of Islam. To bring Muslims back to the true faith, bin Laden believed that the *umma* had to return to a strict and literal interpretation of Islam based on *Sharia*, or Islamic law. He wanted to see things as he believed they had been in the first decades after Islam was founded, during the seventh century. At that time the Arab Muslims were conquering neighboring lands, which were ruled as a theocracy by a religious and political figure called the caliph.

Sometime around the summer of 1988, bin Laden began to collaborate with members of an Egyptian fundamentalist group called Islamic Jihad. During the 1980s this organization had been involved in terrorist attacks meant to overthrow the secular Egyptian government and replace it with Islamic rule. One of the most notorious of these attacks was the 1981 assassination of Egyptian president Anwar Sadat, who had signed a peace treaty with Israel

Al-Qaeda leaders Osama bin Laden (left) and Ayman al-Zawahiri in Afghanistan during the 1990s.

that was highly controversial in the Arab world.

Islamic Jihad was led by an Egyptian doctor named Ayman al-Zawahiri. As Muslim fundamentalists, Zawahiri and Osama bin Laden shared common goals. Both wanted to rid the Muslim world of what they considered to be the destructive influence of western nations like the United States. They believed that they could use modern technology and terrorist tactics to weaken and overthrow secular governments in Muslim lands to recreate the Islamic caliphate.

The new organization they created became known as al-Qaeda. This name, Arabic for "the base," referred to the work bin Laden had done building bases for the *mujahideen* in Afghanistan.

Al-Qaeda was, and is, not organized in the same manner as most other terrorist groups, because from the beginning it operated with the goal of uniting Muslims from many countries. The organization welcomed extremists from numerous countries in the Middle East and central Asia. Even disaffected American, British, and French Muslims could embrace al-Qaeda's ideology, making it a truly global terrorist network. Because of its international approach, al-Qaeda developed strong ties to Islamist groups that operated in specific countries. These included Jemaah Islamiyah (JI) in Indonesia; the Armed Islamic Group (AIG) in Algeria; the Abu Sayyaf Group in the Philippines; Islamic Jihad in Egypt; and Hamas in the Gaza Strip, among others. Members of these groups were invited to attend training camps operated by al-Qaeda, where would-be terrorists were taught how to make bombs and use weapons.

Unlike other groups, bin Laden and other al-Qaeda leaders did not simply issue orders for activities and programs, that were carried out by lower-level members of the group. Instead, the organization developed small groups of between three and 20 people, called cells, in many countries. These groups would propose operations to bin Laden and other top al-Qaeda leaders. If the leadership approved, al-Qaeda would provide funding and help with planning terrorist attacks.

Members of the different cells all worked on different projects, and generally did not know about the activities of other al-Qaeda cells. This way, if police captured some of the terrorists, they would not gain information from them that would enable authorities to prevent other plots from moving forward.

The group's activities did not draw much attention at first, as U.S. leaders were more focused on pressing threats elsewhere. In July 1990 Iraq had invaded the small neighboring country of Kuwait, seizing control of its oil fields. American leaders feared that Saudi Arabia, with its own rich oil fields, would be the next Arab state to fall. At the request of the Saudi monarchy, the U.S. immediately sent troops to defend the kingdom from attack.

This move angered Islamists like bin Laden. Saudi Arabia is home to several of Islam's most important shrines, particularly the city of Mecca, which Muslims regard as the holiest place in the world. Historically, "infidels," or people who do not follow Islam, were not permitted to set foot in Mecca, so Muslim fundamentalists were offended that non-Muslim American soldiers were camped in the Arabian desert to defend the kingdom. Bin Laden offered to raise an army of Arab *mujahideen* that would protect Saudi Arabia from invasion. The Saudi king rebuffed the offer. American troops, along with soldiers from many other countries, would eventually drive Iraq out of Kuwait in the 1991 Gulf War.

The fact that U.S. troops remained in Saudi Arabia even after the Gulf War ended angered bin Laden, as well as many other Arabs. The American soldiers had stayed to make sure that Iraq's dictator, Saddam Hussein, complied with a United Nations requirement to dismantle the country's weapons of mass destruction. However, bin Laden began to publicly criticize the Saudi ruling family, claiming it was corrupt and not religious. He encouraged Muslims to rise up and overthrow the ruling family. At the same time, al-Qaeda secretly planned and launched terrorist attacks aimed at destabilizing the Saudi regime. It is likely that al-Qaeda was also involved in several bombings at U.S. military facilities in Saudi Arabia during the mid-1990s. However, al-Qaeda did not take public credit for these attacks, so it

remained an enemy that few Americans knew about.

From 1992 to 1996, bin Laden directed terrorist operations from the African country of Sudan, which had an Islamist government that had granted him sanctuary. However, after several attacks the Saudi ruling family pressured Sudan's government to expel him from the country. Bin Laden was forced to leave Sudan. He returned to a familiar place—Afghanistan.

When the Soviets had pulled out in 1989, Afghanistan had collapsed into civil war, with various *mujahideen* groups fighting for control of the country. By

U.S. Marines disembark from a transport at Dhahran, Saudi Arabia, in September 1990. The arrival of more than 500,000 U.S. troops in Saudi Arabia, intended to protect the kingdom from invasion by Iraq, angered many Muslims, especially fundamentalists like Osama bin Laden.

CASE FILE

Name: Osama bin Laden

Born: March 10, 1957, in Saudi Arabia

Location of Attacks: Afghanistan, Indonesia, Iraq, Kenya, Pakistan, the Philippines, Saudi Arabia, Tanzania, Turkey, the United Kingdom, United States, Yemen

Number of victims: more than 4,000 killed; thousands of others injured

Modus Operandi: as head of the al-Qaeda network, authorized and financed bombings, hijackings, assassinations, and other attacks

Justice: killed by US Navy SEALs in Abbottabad, Pakistan, on May 2, 2011; buried at sea.

1996 an Islamist group called the Taliban had largely gained control. This was an ideal situation for bin Laden. In the rural mountains of Afghanistan he could train terrorists without fear of being harassed. Also, the fundamentalist Taliban regime represented the type of Islamic society that bin Laden wanted to create elsewhere in the Muslim world.

After re-establishing his base in Afghanistan, in August 1996 bin Laden issued a public statement calling on Muslims to kill Americans and Jews. The statement was worded in the style of a *fatwa*, or ruling on Islamic law, and was originally published in an Arabic-language newspaper in London. "There is no more important duty than pushing the American enemy out of the holy land," wrote bin Laden. Addressing American soldiers, he wrote:

> Terrorising you, while you are carrying arms on our land, is a legitimate and morally demanded duty. It is a legitimate right well known to all humans and other creatures. Your example and our example is like a snake which entered into a house of a man and got killed by him. . . .
>
> It is a duty now on every tribe in the Arab Peninsula to fight, Jihad, in the cause of Allah and to cleanse the land from those occupiers.

Bin Laden's 1996 *fatwa* was largely ignored. At the time, few Americans knew about the existence of al-Qaeda. Two years later, in February 1998, bin Laden issued another *fatwa*, declaring war against the United States and Israel. This statement was signed by members of other Islamist terrorist groups, including the Egyptian Islamic Group, Jamiat-ul-Ulama-e-Pakistan, and the Jihad Movement in Bangladesh. The *fatwa* stated:

> To kill the Americans and their allies— civilians and military—is an individual duty for every Muslim who can do it in any country in which it is possible to do it, in order to liberate the al-Aqsa Mosque [in Jerusalem] and the holy mosque [in Mecca] from their grip, and in order for their armies to move out of all the lands of Islam, defeated and unable to threaten any Muslim.

Again, the *fatwa* attracted little attention among most Americans at

U.S. Secretary of Defense William S. Cohen (left) and General Henry Shelton brief reporters on the U.S. military strike on a factory in Sudan and terrorist training camps in Afghanistan, August 20, 1998. Cohen said the cruise missile attacks were "part of a continuing effort to defend U.S. citizens and interests abroad against the very real threat posed by international terrorists. We've taken these actions to reduce the ability of these terrorist organizations to train and equip their misguided followers or to acquire weapons of mass destruction for their use in campaigns of terror."

first. That would change six months later, when al-Qaeda terrorists detonated bombs outside the U.S. embassies in Kenya and Tanzania. Together, these attacks killed more than 220 people and injured nearly 4,600.

This attack finally drew a U.S. response—about two weeks later, cruise missiles were fired at four of al-Qaeda's terrorist camps in Afghanistan as well as at a pharmaceutical plant in Sudan that the American government suspected was being used by al-Qaeda to make chemical weapons. American military leaders had hoped bin Laden would be killed in this strike, but it turned out that he had left one of the camps a few hours before the missiles hit.

Osama bin Laden vowed that he would strike at the United States again. Al-Qaeda planned a new series of attacks for New Year's Day of the year 2000. The group was going to detonate bombs and release poison gas at airports and tourist sites in Jordan, and bomb Los Angeles International Airport in the United States. It also wanted to try to sink a U.S. warship in the harbor at Aden, Yemen. Ultimately, none of these attacks came to pass. Jordanian police caught the terrorist cell that was planning the airport bombings in that country. American authorities arrested an Algerian man who was trying to smuggle explosives into the U.S., and broke up another al-Qaeda cell. In Yemen, the terrorists loaded so much explosive into a small boat that it sank before it could reach the American warship, USS *The Sullivans*.

Eight months later, al-Qaeda would give their warship attack plan another

This view of the USS *Cole*'s port side shows the large hole in the side of the ship caused by a terrorist bomb while the *Cole* was in Aden harbor, October 2000. The attack killed 17 U.S. sailors.

try, and this time things would go much differently. On October 12, 2000, an American warship, the USS *Cole*, was in Aden harbor to take on fuel and supplies when it was approached by a small boat carrying two men. Although the *Cole*'s sailors warned the men to stay away, the two men smiled and waved as their boat pulled up next to the warship. Then one of the men detonated a bomb, which blew a gaping hole in the side of the *Cole*. The two suicide bombers were killed, along with 17 American sailors. Dozens of other sailors were injured.

By this time, al-Qaeda cells in the United States were planning an even bigger attack. In 1999 Bin Laden and other al-Qaeda leaders—including Khaled Sheikh Mohammed, who had joined the organization in 1998—had selected a small group of terrorists who

could speak fluent English and were capable of learning to fly a large commercial jet airplane. They included Mohammed Atta, Marwan al-Shehhi, and Ziad Jarrah. These three men entered the United States in 2000 and enrolled in flight training school in Florida. Others—including Hani Hanjour, who had already been a trained pilot when he joined al-Qaeda—came into the United States during 2001. Targets were chosen: the World Trade Center in New York City, the Pentagon in Arlington, Virginia, and either the White House or the U.S. Capitol building in Washington, D.C. (Because this attack failed, the final target is uncertain, although al-Qaeda terrorists captured afterward have said that both were considered. Bin Laden is said to have preferred the Capitol, because he thought the White House would be harder to find from the air.) U.S. authorities later estimated that the plot cost between $400,000 and $500,000, most of which was provided by al-Qaeda.

On the morning of September 11, 2001, the terrorists carried out their devastating attack against the United States. Although American leaders initially thought that Iraq might have been responsible, evidence soon emerged that indicated bin Laden and al-Qaeda had been behind the attack.

U.S. President George W. Bush demanded that Afghanistan's Taliban government hand over bin Laden. When the Taliban refused, the United States and some of its allies attacked Afghanistan. The war, which began in October 2001, was intended to topple the Taliban regime and capture the terrorists. The U.S. worked with Afghan groups that were opposed to the Taliban, known as the Northern Alliance. By the end of 2001, the Taliban had been forced from power, the al-Qaeda terrorist training camps had been destroyed, and many terrorists had been captured. However, bin Laden, Zawahiri, and other top leaders

New York City firefighters work near the area known as Ground Zero after the collapse of the Twin Towers September 11, 2001 in New York City.

WANTED: DEAD OR ALIVE

After the 1998 embassy bombings in Kenya and Tanzania, the U.S. government made catching Osama bin Laden a priority. After the terrorist leader was indicted by a U.S. court for his involvement in the attacks, he was placed on the FBI's Most Wanted list, and a $10 million reward was offered for his capture.

On August 20, 1998, President Bill Clinton authorized cruise missile strikes against al-Qaeda's facilities near Khost, Afghanistan. The military hoped that bin Laden would be killed in the attack, but he had left the area a few hours before the missiles arrived. In 1999 and 2000, the Central Intelligence Agency (CIA) arranged for foreign operatives to try to kill bin Laden, but these attempts failed.

After the September 11, 2001, terrorist attack, the search for bin Laden intensified. During an interview with CNN six days after the attack, U.S. President George W. Bush said of Osama bin Laden, "I want justice, and there's an old poster out West I recall, that said, 'Wanted, Dead or Alive.'" The reward for the al-Qaeda leader was soon increased to $25 million. American troops had a chance to capture or kill bin Laden at the battle of Tora Bora in Afghanistan during November 2001, but bin Laden was able to slip away.

Over the next decade, bin Laden remained in hiding, sending taped messages to his followers from an unknown location. Many rumors circulated about bin Laden's whereabouts, but the U.S. was unable to track the al-Qaeda leader. In 2007, the reward for his capture was increased to $50 million.

MURDER OF U.S. NATIONALS OUTSIDE THE UNITED STATES; CONSPIRACY TO MURDER U.S. NATIONALS OUTSIDE THE UNITED STATES; ATTACK ON A FEDERAL FACILITY RESULTING IN DEATH

USAMA BIN LADEN

Aliases: Usama Bin Muhammad Bin Ladin, Shaykh Usama Bin Ladin, The Prince, The Emir, Abu Abdallah, Mujahid Shaykh, Hajj, The Director

DESCRIPTION

Date of Birth Used:	1957	**Hair:**	Brown
Place of Birth:	Saudi Arabia	**Eyes:**	Brown
Height:	6'4" to 6'6"	**Sex:**	Male
Weight:	Approximately 160 pounds	**Complexion:**	Olive
Build:	Thin	**Citizenship:**	Saudi Arabian
Language:	Arabic (probably Pashtu)		
Scars and Marks:	None known		
Remarks:	Bin Laden is left-handed and walks with a cane.		

CAUTION

Usama Bin Laden is wanted in connection with the August 7, 1998, bombings of the United States Embassies in Dar es Salaam, Tanzania, and Nairobi, Kenya. These attacks killed over 200 people. In addition, Bin Laden is a suspect in other terrorist attacks throughout the world.

REWARD

The Rewards For Justice Program, United States Department of State, is offering a reward of up to $25 million for information leading directly to the apprehension or conviction of Usama Bin Laden. An additional $2 million is being offered through a program developed and funded by the Airline Pilots Association and the Air Transport Association.

SHOULD BE CONSIDERED ARMED AND DANGEROUS

IF YOU HAVE ANY INFORMATION CONCERNING THIS PERSON, PLEASE CONTACT YOUR LOCAL FBI OFFICE **OR THE NEAREST** AMERICAN EMBASSY OR CONSULATE.

of al-Qaeda had managed to slip away, using the network of tunnels that had been built during the Soviet-Afghan conflict.

Though bin Laden had escaped, the U.S. invasion of Afghanistan severely handicapped al-Qaeda's ability to launch new terrorist attacks. The group had lost its training facilities, and its leaders were forced to hide out. The U.S. government launched a global effort to cut off al-Qaeda's funding sources and arrest or kill its leaders.

Several key members of the organization were captured during the 2001 fighting in Afghanistan. Other high-ranking al-Qaeda members were caught in Pakistan during 2002 and 2003. These included Abu Zubaydah, who ran al-Qaeda terrorist training camps, and Mustafa al-Hawsawi, a Saudi who had wired funds to the September 11 terrorists. The terrorists were interrogated, and often tortured, by American officials in order to get information that would enable them to prevent future al-Qaeda terrorist attacks.

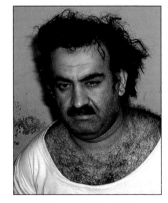

Khaled Sheikh
Mohammed

In March 2003, a senior al-Qaeda operative named Khaled Sheikh Mohammed was captured in Pakistan. After a lengthy interrogation, he confessed to being the mastermind of the September 11 plot and provided details about other al-Qaeda activities. Mohammed, like other high-level terrorists, was held in a special high-security prison at the U.S. military base at Guantanamo Bay, Cuba.

Despite the loss of many senior members, al-Qaeda continued to plan attacks, although it often had to work with foreign Islamist groups to carry them out. Bin Laden released messages on videotape or cassette tape exhorting Muslims to join al-Qaeda's jihad. These messages were uploaded to the Internet and broadcast on the Arab television network Al-Jazeera in order to attract and inspire new terrorists.

For example, on October 12, 2002, members of Jemaah Islamiyah carried out a bomb attack at a tourist resort on the Indonesian island of Bali. Three bombs were detonated, killing 202 people and injuring more than 240. Many of the victims were Australian civilians. It was the deadliest terrorist attack in Indonesia's history. A week later, Al-Jazeera aired a tape in which bin Laden claimed the attack was in retaliation for Australia's support of the United States and for its involvement in East Timor, a former Indonesian province that had become independent in 1999.

In March 2003 the United States and some of its allies invaded Iraq, and quickly overthrew the dictator Saddam Hussein. Conflict and chaos followed as various factions in Iraq struggled for power. Among them was an Islamist group calling itself al-Qaeda in Mesopotamia, which launched terrorist attacks against American troops as well as Kurds and Shiite Muslims in Iraq. It was led by a Jordanian militant named Abu Musab al-Zarqawi. Among the group's most deadly attacks was a series of near-simultaneous bombings in August 2003 that killed 23 people, including a high-ranking United Nations diplomat named Sérgio Vieira de Mello, at the UN headquarters in Baghdad, Iraq's capital; 17 people at Jordan's embassy in Baghdad; and 86 worshippers at a Shiite mosque in the city of Najaf. In 2004, al-Qaeda in Iraq detonated bombs that killed nearly 180 Shiites on the Muslim holy day of Ashura.

Zarqawi's attacks were planned to increase tension between Shiites and Sunni Muslims in Iraq. The group's leaders hoped that Iraq would collapse into civil war between the major religious and ethnic factions: Shiite Muslims, Sunni Muslims, and Kurds. Eventually, though, American troops and Iraqi police were able to kill Zarqawi and reduce the level of violence in Iraq.

On July 7, 2005, al-Qaeda showed that it could still strike in western nations. That morning, four British Muslim suicide bombers detonated bombs on subway trains and a bus in London, killing 56 people and injuring more than 700. The group publicly claimed credit for the attack, and investigators later found evidence that showed

The ruins of the Canal Hotel in Baghdad, Iraq, where an al-Qaeda bomb killed 23 people and wounded more than 100 others in August 2003. The building housed the headquarters of the United Nations in Iraq. The U.N. special ambassador, Sérgio Vieira de Mello, was among those killed in the terrorist attack.

Ambulances respond to the scene of one of the terrorist bombings on London's public transportation system, July 7, 2005. This al-Qaeda attack was the deadliest terrorist incident in London's history.

al-Qaeda leaders had helped to plan the bombings. British police were able to arrest several members of the terrorist cell within a few weeks of the attack.

That year, the CIA secretly began a new program aimed at eliminating al-Qaeda's leaders around the world. Unmanned aircraft equipped with high-resolution cameras and powerful missiles, called Predator drones, were used to observe areas where terrorists were suspected to be hiding, such as in the region along the border between Afghanistan and northwest Pakistan. The drones could fly up to two miles above a target, so they could spy on suspects without being detected. When a terrorist was identified, the drone could fire its missiles at the enemy.

The U.S. military had previously used Predator drones against both military targets and terrorists in Iraq, Afghanistan, and other countries. In 2002, for example, a military drone destroyed a car carrying Qaed Salim Sinan al-Harethi, one of the terrorists suspected of planning the 2000 *Cole* bombing. However, the expanded CIA program drew criticism because at times Pakistani civilians were accidentally killed by drone missile attacks. Nonetheless, American leaders continued both the military and the CIA Predator drone programs because of their successes. In 2005, several important al-Qaeda leaders were killed by drones operating over Pakistan. One was Abu Hamza Rabia, the organization's third-highest ranking member after bin Laden and Zawahiri.

The drone attacks took a major toll on al-Qaeda, with leaders of the group

A U.S. Predator drone searches for al-Qaeda terrorists over Afghanistan.

complaining that terrorists were being killed faster than new ones could be recruited. In December 2007, al-Qaeda assassinated Benazir Bhutto, a former prime minister of Pakistan. The terrorist who plotted and carried out this attack, Baitullah Mehsud, was killed by a Predator drone strike in 2009. The drone attacks forced terrorists to be more careful, and restricted their movements.

Still, the organization continued to sow terrorism around the world. In June 2008, a car bomb exploded outside the Danish embassy in Pakistan, killing eight people and injuring 27. A message from al-Qaeda said this bombing was because troops from Denmark were assisting the United States in Afghanistan. In September 2008, terrorists detonated a truck bomb outside a Marriott hotel in Islamabad, Pakistan,

killing 54 people and injuring more than 260 others. This attack had been aimed at several key members of Pakistan's government. They were going to have dinner at the hotel, but had changed their plans at the last minute.

On Christmas day in 2009, an al-Qaeda terrorist named Umar Farouk Abdulmutallab tried to detonate a bomb that he had concealed in his underwear when he boarded Northwest Airlines Flight 253 in Amsterdam. He had been hoping to bring down the aircraft, which was carrying 290 passengers and crew to Detroit. Passengers subdued the bomber before he could set off the explosive, and he was arrested. Investigators later determined that an al-Qaeda regional commander named Anwar al-Aulaqi had inspired the plot.

Five months later, another attack inspired by al-Aulaqi was foiled when a homemade car bomb in New York City's Times Square failed to explode. Police soon arrested Faisal Shahzad, a 30-year-old American citizen of Pakistani descent, as he was trying to escape from the country. Shahzad was tried and sentenced to life in prison.

To many counter-terrorism experts, these failed attacks indicated that al-Qaeda no longer posed much of a threat to Americans. While the group could still inspire militants to attempt terrorist attacks, it no longer had the resources to plan, finance, and carry out the sort of ambitious, daring plots that al-Qaeda had once been known for. The decade-long U.S. campaign against al-Qaeda had eliminated most of the group's safe havens and financing. Al-Qaeda's last successful attack in a western country had come in 2005. Since then, hundreds of the experts needed to build bombs, and many of the charismatic leaders who could inspire young Muslims to become suicide bombers, had been killed.

Al-Qaeda suffered its biggest loss in the spring of 2011, when U.S. Navy SEALs made a daring raid on a compound in Abbotabad, Pakistan. A few months earlier the CIA had learned that Osama bin Laden might be hiding at the fortified three-story house. The CIA secretly watched the compound until American leaders, including President Barack Obama, were confident that the al-Qaeda chief was living there.

On May 2, 2011, the SEALs were secretly flown to the compound by helicopter. They broke in and began to search for bin Laden, killing al-Qaeda guards who tried to protect the leader. The SEALs found Bin Laden on the third floor of the compound, and shot him when he did not immediately surrender. The SEALs took the corpse, along with bin Laden's computer and papers, and some members of his family who were captured, and escaped by helicopter. The entire raid took only about 40 minutes.

Bin Laden's body was flown to an American aircraft carrier in the Persian Gulf. There, the terrorist mastermind's body was prepared for burial according to Muslim rites, and was buried at sea the day after he was killed. This was done because no government of a Muslim country would accept his body for burial, and also so that his grave could not become a shrine for Islamists.

American experts with the FBI and CIA analyzed information from bin Laden's cell phones, computers, and other documents. They used this data to capture or kill many of the remaining al-Qaeda leaders. One of them was Atiyah Abd al-Rahman, a longtime bin Laden associate who became al-Qaeda's second-in-command when Ayman al Zawahiri advanced to the top leadership spot after bin Laden's death. Al-Rahman was killed in Pakistan by a drone strike in August 2011. Another leader, Anwar al-Aulaqi, was killed in Yemen by a drone strike in September 2011.

Today, most American experts believe al-Qaeda is on the run. But the group, though smaller, still exists, and it remains dangerous because of the inspiration it continues to provide to Islamist insurgent groups in many Arab and Muslim countries in the Middle East, North Africa, and Asia. The hunt for Ayman al-Zawahiri continues, with the U.S. offering a $25 million reward for his capture.

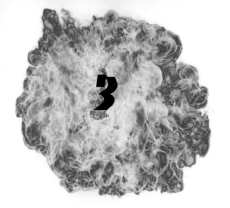

AUM SHINRIKYO
TERROR IN TOKYO

Throughout recorded history, humans have worried about the end of the world. During the 1990s, as the western world approached the start of a new millennium, a number of people feared that the year 2000 would mark the start of the apocalypse. Some of them decided to prepare for the end by joining religious cults with others who believed the same things.

In Japan, members of a fringe religious order called Aum Shinrikyo did not just believe that the world was soon going to end. They felt it was their responsibility to help bring the apocalypse about through their own violent actions. In the spring of 1995, this misguided belief would lead to the deadliest terrorist attack in Japanese history.

The Aum Shinrikyo cult was founded in the late 1980s by a man named Chizuo Matsumoto. He had been born partially blind into a poor family. As an

adult, Matsumoto operated a folk medicine shop and taught yoga. Like most Japanese he was a Buddhist, although he later studied Christianity and Hinduism. In 1987 Matsumoto changed his name to Shoko Asahara and declared himself head of a new religious order, Aum Shinrikyo. It incorporated Buddhist, Christian, and Hindu beliefs along with Asahara's own teachings.

The name combines the sacred Hindu word *aum*, which is considered to represent the powers of creation and destruction in the universe, and the Japanese word *shinrikyo*, meaning "religion of truth." (In English, Aum Shinrikyo is usually translated as "Supreme Truth.") Asahara preached that the end of the world was near, and claimed that only Aum Shinrikyo followers would survive the coming apocalypse.

Shoko Asahara presented himself as a god-like figure and imposed strict rules on his followers. He insisted that they should turn over their material possessions to the cult and isolate themselves from the outside world. Followers were ordered to abandon family members who did not practice the religion.

The teachings of Shoko Asahara appealed to some young Japanese who were disillusioned by the materialism of Japanese society. By the early 1990s Aum Shinrikyo was the fastest-growing religious sect in Japan.

In 1989 Aum Shinrikyo was granted the status of a legal religion in Japan. This made it exempt from taxes, and enabled the group to accumulate great wealth by operating businesses and restaurants. However, the government decision to grant tax-exempt status was controversial, as by this time some people were concerned that Aum Shinrikyo was a dangerous cult. They believed Asahara exploited members for his own benefit. These suspicions increased when a lawyer named Sakamato Tsutsumi, who was working on a lawsuit against Aum Shinrikyo, disappeared along with his wife and infant child in 1989. It would later turn out that they had been murdered by members of the sect, who wanted to prevent him from revealing embarrassing information about Aum Shinrikyo.

This was not the only incident. Japanese police later uncovered evidence of 33 murders committed by

CASE FILE

Name: Chizuo Matsumoto

Alias: Shoko Asahara

Born: March 2, 1955

Location of Attacks: Tokyo, Japan

Number of victims: 27 killed, thousands more injured in multiple gas attacks

Modus Operandi: use of sarin gas

Captured: May 1995

Justice: Convicted in 2004 on 13 of 17 indictments for murder and sentenced to death by hanging. Appeals for a new trial have been denied, although the execution has been postponed several times due to other Aum Shinrikyo cases

members of the group between 1988 and March 1995. Most of these attacks targeted people who were about to leave Aum Shinrikyo. Some researchers believe the actual number of murders committed by Aum Shinrikyo members during this time may be 80 or more.

In 1990, Asahara decided to seek a seat in Japan's parliament, along with 25 other members of Aum Shinrikyo. All were badly defeated in the elections. After this, Asahara apparently decided that if he could not take over the Japanese government through the electoral process, he would do so by violent means. Aum Shinrikyo soon constructed a secret factory to produce chemical and biological weapons.

To justify the religion's use of violence, Shoko Asahara preached a twisted version of a Buddhist concept called *poa*. In traditional Buddhist thought, *poa* involves the transferring of consciousness to a higher level at the time of death. However, according to Shoko Asahara's version of

Shoko Asahara

poa, killing those who opposed Aum Shinrikyo would bring about the salvation of those people, because they would be reborn after the predicted apocalypse. In other words, Asahara told his followers to kill people so that they could be saved.

In 1993 members of Aum Shinrikyo attempted to spread anthrax in Tokyo. Anthrax is a bacteria that can be deadly when used as a biological weapon. However, the form of anthrax that was used was weak, so their attempted terrorist attack went unnoticed.

By then, however, Aum Shinrikyo was moving on to an even more toxic weapon. In 1993 an Aum Shinrikyo member named Masami Tsuchiya, who was a chemist, managed to produce sarin, a deadly nerve agent, in the cult's secret laboratory. Sarin had originally been developed by Nazi scientists during the 1930s, and was banned by the United Nations as a weapon of mass destruction. Sarin prevents a person

from breathing by paralyzing the respiratory system. A single drop the size of a pinhead can be deadly.

In June 1994, members of Aum Shinrikyo released sarin gas around the town of Matsumoto, Japan. Eight people were killed and over 200 were harmed by the gas. Initially, no one realized that Aum Shinrikyo was responsible. Instead, an innocent local farmer was arrested and blamed.

Aum Shinrikyo had committed the Matsumoto attack for two reasons. First, they were hoping the gas would kill some judges who were scheduled to rule on a legal matter about property owned by Aum Shinrikyo in the Matsumoto area. Second, it was a trial run for an even more spectacular attack planned by the group.

On the morning of March 20, 1995, members of Aum Shinrikyo released packages containing sarin on five subway trains in different areas of Tokyo, the Japanese capital. It was the busiest time on the subway, as millions of commuters were heading to their jobs. Within hours, more than 5,000 people were affected enough by the sarin gas to require hospital care. Thirteen were killed, while 50 others suffered serious injuries. It was the worst terrorist attack in Japan's history.

Workers clean toxic sarin gas from the Tokyo subway system, March 1995.

The police soon found Aum Shinrikyo's secret chemical weapons factory, as well as plenty of evidence that implicated the cult in the Tokyo subway attack and the Matsumoto incident. Clearly, other attacks were planned, as the laboratory contained the ingredients for enough sarin to kill millions of people.

Shoko Asahara and more than 180 Aum Shinrikyo members were arrested. Prosecutors charged that Asahara had ordered the attacks hoping to overthrow the Japanese government and bring about a world war. Although he pled "not guilty," Asahara was convicted in 2004 and sentenced to death by hanging. Twelve other top-ranking members of Aum Shinrikyo were sentenced to death, five received life sentences, and 167 received prison sentences of varying lengths.

The Aum Shinrikyo religion still exists, although its current leaders have officially renounced violence. The organization's activities are carefully regulated by the Japanese government, and it is no longer considered a threat.

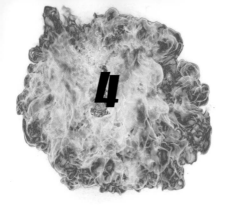

CARLOS THE JACKAL
TERRORIST FOR HIRE

Carlos the Jackal was the most famous terrorist of the 1970s and 1980s. He was involved in attacks throughout Europe, many of which were committed in the name of Palestinian liberation. However, Carlos was a revolutionary-for-hire, who employed his skills as a terrorist on behalf of many different organizations against the established governments of the time.

To some, the shadowy Carlos was a glamorous figure who was able to pull off amazing capers, then elude authorities. His nickname "the Jackal" came from a popular 1971 novel about a charismatic but deadly assassin titled *The Day of the Jackal*; police had once found a copy of the book among belongings Carlos had left behind while escaping capture. Others saw him as a ruthless murderer who killed at least 80 people through his terrorist activities over 25 years.

The terrorist known as Carlos the Jackal was born Ilich Ramírez Sánchez in Venezuela during October 1949. His father was a Communist, and as a child Ilich (named for Vladimir Ilich Lenin, the Communist revolutionary and first leader of the Soviet Union) embraced Marxist teachings. When he was 10 he joined the youth division of the Venezuelan Communist Party.

In 1966, the teenage Ilich Ramírez reportedly spent a summer in Cuba, where he received training in guerrilla warfare. Two years later, Ramírez enrolled at a university in Moscow. He left school in 1970 and traveled to the Middle Eastern country of Lebanon.

Lebanon borders the state of Israel, and at that time was the home of many refugees who had left Palestine in 1947 when Israel was founded. There, Ramírez joined the Popular Front for the Liberation of Palestine (PFLP), an organization that embraced Communist ideology and had as its goal the destruction of Israel and the creation of a Palestinian state. The Palestinian officer who recruited Ramírez gave him the code-name "Carlos," to reflect his Latin American origin. Carlos trained in a PFLP camp located in Jordan, until that country's military forced the organization to leave. Carlos moved to London, where he worked secretly for the PFLP.

By 1975, Carlos had participated in several attempted terrorist attacks in England and France. Most of these failed. In June 1975, three French intelligence agents, tipped off that Carlos had been involved in some of the failed attacks, attempted to question him at a house in Paris. Carlos shot the three agents, killing two of them, and escaped to Beirut, the capital of Lebanon.

In Beirut, Carlos helped to plan a daring attack on the headquarters of the Organization of Petroleum Exporting Countries (OPEC) in Vienna, Austria. The target was unexpected—many of the major Arab states that were sympathetic to the Palestinian cause and supported the PFLP were also members of OPEC, a cartel that helps to set the international price of oil by controlling the amount produced by member nations.

On the morning of December 21, 1975, Carlos led a six-person team into OPEC headquarters. They killed two security guards and a Libyan economist,

CASE FILE

Name: Ilich Ramírez Sánchez

Alias: Carlos the Jackal

Born: October 12, 1949

Location of Attacks: Austria, England, France, Holland, Jordan, Libya, others not confirmed.

Number of victims: at least 80

Modus Operandi: bombings, rocket attacks, armed kidnapping.

Captured: August 14, 1994.

Justice: Convicted in 1997 of murdering two French intelligence agents and sentenced to life imprisonment; convicted in 2011 of bombings in France that killed 11 and injured 145, and sentenced to a second life term.

and took more than 70 people hostage, including the oil ministers of 11 OPEC member countries. A shootout with police ended in a standoff and a 36-hour siege. The purpose of the raid was to raise awareness of the Palestinian cause, so Carlos threatened to kill one hostage every 15 minutes unless Austrian radio and television networks broadcast his anti-Israel and pro-Palestinian statement every two hours.

The Austrian government gave in to this demand. The next day, the Austrian government acquiesced to another demand, providing Carlos and his cohorts an airplane so they could fly from Vienna to Algiers, the capital of Algeria. Carlos freed some of the hostages, but

For many years this was one of the few photos that authorities had of the mysterious terrorist known as Carlos the Jackal.

took 42 hostages on the airplane, flying first to Algiers, then to Tripoli, Libya, then back to Algiers. There, the remaining hostages were freed. Among them were two oil ministers that Carlos had specifically been ordered to kill by his PFLP superiors: Ahmed Zaki Yamani of Saudi Arabia and Jamshid Amuzegar of Iran. However, Carlos released them unharmed when he was personally paid more than $20 million by the Iranian and Saudi governments. Carlos was also rewarded by Libyan ruler Muammar Gaddafi, who gave the terrorist sanctuary in Tripoli.

Although Carlos turned over some of the ransom money to the PFLP, he was kicked out of the group for failing to execute the ministers. However, the PFLP used their share of the ransom, at least $10 million, to finance other attacks, including the hijacking of an Air France jet to Entebbe, Uganda, in 1976.

By the late 1970s, Carlos had settled in the Communist country of East Germany. There, he planned terrorist attacks on various targets in Europe. These included bombing the office of Radio Free Europe in Munich, West Germany, in 1981; an attempt to launch rockets at a French nuclear power plant in 1982; and detonating bombs on two French high-speed trains in 1983.

Carlos was daring and charismatic. He often sent letters to news agencies taking credit for his attacks. Although a notorious criminal, he also became something of a celebrity in Europe. Rumors swirled about the most wanted man on the continent, who supposedly spent the proceeds from his terrorist attacks on wild parties and gambling.

To avoid arrest, Carlos was forced to move from country to country. He spent time in several Communist countries in eastern Europe. Eventually, he returned to the Middle East, settling in Syria for several years. The Syrian government agreed to let him stay as long as he was not actively involved in terrorism. This kept Carlos quiet for several years.

In 1990, the government of Iraq approached Carlos about restarting his terrorist activities. In September 1991, after Iraq was defeated in the Gulf War, the Syrian government expelled Carlos. He found sanctuary in Sudan, an African state with an Islamist government that harbored other terrorists at the time, including Osama bin Laden.

During the early 1990s, the French and U.S. governments sought to have Carlos extradited from Sudan so that he could be placed on trial for his terrorist crimes. In 1992, Carlos was convicted *in absentia* by the French government for the murders of the two French intelligence agents in 1975. (A trial *in absentia* is one in which the person accused of a crime is not physically present.)

Sudan initially resisted pressure to extradite the terrorist, but Carlos's playboy lifestyle eventually became an embarrassment. Islamic law, or *Sharia*, was the basis of Sudan's legal system, and Carlos's partying and gambling offended many Muslims. In August 1994 Sudan's government allowed Carlos to be arrested by French police and taken to France.

In December 1997, Carlos was placed on trial in Paris for the 1975 agent murders. He was convicted and sentenced to life imprisonment.

From 1994 until 2002, Carlos was held in solitary confinement at the La Santé high-security prison in France. He remains at the prison. In late 2011, Carlos was placed on trial a second time for four of the bombings he had masterminded in France during the 1980s. Those attacked had killed 11 people and injured 145. The 62-year-old terrorist was convicted in December 2011 and given a second life sentence.

In prison, Carlos the Jackal remains unrepentant of his crimes.

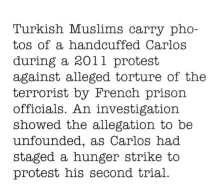

Turkish Muslims carry photos of a handcuffed Carlos during a 2011 protest against alleged torture of the terrorist by French prison officials. An investigation showed the allegation to be unfounded, as Carlos had staged a hunger strike to protest his second trial.

HEZBOLLAH
THE POLITICS OF TERROR

On the morning of October 23, 1983, guards outside the U.S. Marine barracks in Beirut, Lebanon, observed a large yellow truck approaching along the highway toward the airport. It was nothing to be concerned about—the truck made regular deliveries of fresh water to the base. However, the truck suddenly swung off the road, crashed through a gate, veered around a wall of sandbags, and headed straight toward the barracks entrance. The surprised sentries did not have enough time to stop the truck before it crashed into the barracks building at 6:20 A.M.

An enormous bomb then detonated, creating what FBI investigators would later describe as the "largest non-nuclear blast in history." The Beirut Marine barracks was destroyed, and 241 soldiers were killed. Hundreds more were injured and trapped under the rubble of cement and cinderblocks. In a similar, almost simultaneous, bombing nearby 56 French paratroopers were killed. American newspapers described the incident as the worst sneak attack since Pearl Harbor.

Investigators would later learn that the water truck had been hijacked by terrorists from a group that called itself Islamic Jihad Organization. This group would later change its name to Hezbollah (Arabic for "Party of Allah"), and would become infamous as one of the world's most notorious terrorist organizations.

Hezbollah was formed in 1982 in southern Lebanon. A decade earlier, this small country on the eastern Mediterranean Sea had been among the most cosmopolitan and prosperous countries in the Arab world. But in 1975 the country's various religious and political factions began fighting a bloody civil

(Right) View of the building that U.S. Marines were using as a barracks in Beirut, Lebanon, in 1983.

(Bottom) Ruins of the barracks building, which was destroyed by Hezbollah terrorists in October 1983. The deadly truck bombing was a success for the terrorists, as the American peacekeeping forces soon withdrew from Lebanon.

war. By 1982 Lebanon was considered to be one of the most dangerous and unstable places in the world, and U.S. Marines had been sent to help keep the peace.

The founders of Hezbollah were Muslims. They followed a branch of the religion known as Shia Islam, and were called Shiites. Shia Islam is the smaller of the two major sects of Islam; follow-ers of the larger sect are called Sunni Muslims. Lebanon is one of the few countries where there are more Shiites than Sunnis. However, in Lebanon the Shiites historically were mostly poor farmers, and as a group they had less political power than either the country's Sunni Muslims or Lebanese followers of other religions, such as the Druze or Maronite Christians.

(Left) The fertile Beqaa Valley is home to many Lebanese Shiite Muslims.

(Below) In 1979 Ayatollah Khomeini led a Shiite revolution in Iran that established an Islamist government. Under Khomeini's rule, Iran became one of the world's foremost state sponsors of terrorism during the 1980s. It provided arms, funds, training, and sanctuary to Hezbollah, as well as to terrorist groups in Bahrain, Iraq, Saudi Arabia, and other countries.

At the time Hezbollah was organized, the government of Lebanon was paralyzed by the civil war. It had largely abandoned efforts to control southern Lebanon. In the early 1970s armed Palestinian terrorist groups had moved into the region, and these groups had a free hand in southern Lebanon. They used the region as a base from which to launch attacks into Israel, which is located to the south. Israel retaliated in 1978 with a military invasion of Lebanon, intended to drive the Palestinians away from the border. In 1982 Israel launched a second invasion to force the Sunni Muslim Palestinians out of the country. This time, Israeli troops occupied southern Lebanon.

Hezbollah was created with the goal of driving the Israelis out of Lebanon. Another goal of the organization was to establish a government in Lebanon guided by Islamic law and ruled by Shiite clerics.

Hezbollah was supported financially by another country with a Shiite majority, Iran. In 1979 Iranian Islamists had overthrown the country's secular ruler, Reza Shah Pahlavi, and replaced him with a religious theocracy ruled by the Ayatollah Khomeini. Iran was a bitter enemy of the United States, which had long supported the Shah.

Like the Iranians, the founders of Hezbollah also viewed the U.S. and other western nations as enemies because of their support for Israel and because they believed the U.S. troops were in Lebanon to support a Christian

In April 1983, the U.S. Embassy in Beirut was the target of a terrorist bomb that killed 63 people. Most of the victims were embassy staff. It was the deadliest attack on a U.S. diplomatic mission to that point in history.

faction against the Shiites in the civil war.

Hezbollah's first attack (under the name Islamic Jihad) against an American target came on April 18, 1983, when a van loaded with explosives was detonated outside the U.S. Embassy in Beirut. The blast killed 63 people, including 17 Americans. Over the next six months, the U.S. Marines in Beirut faced additional car bombings as well as mortar fire. In response, American warships shelled Shiite camps in the mountains near Beirut. attacks culminating in the October 1983 barracks attack.

After the attack, President Ronald Reagan maintained that terrorists would not drive the U.S. out of Lebanon, but as mortar and grenade attacks continued, the Marines pulled out of Lebanon in May 1984.

Emboldened by this success, Hezbollah continued to wage war against the occupying Israeli army. The organization had bombed the Israeli military headquarters in the Lebanese city of Tyre in 1982 and again in 1983. The two suicide attacks killed about 100 Israeli soldiers and more than 50 Lebanese. By 1985, the constant clashes with Hezbollah militias forced the Israeli army to withdraw from the major cities of southern Lebanon, Sidon and Tyre, as well as from the Beqaa Valley, Lebanon's main agricultural area.

The attacks against American and western targets continued as well. In September 1984, Hezbollah terrorists detonated a bomb at a U.S. Embassy building in East Beirut that killed nine people. The terrorists also turned to a new tactic: kidnapping westerners in

Father Lawrence Jenco (left), a Roman Catholic priest, was held hostage by Hezbollah from January 1985 until July 1986. Terry Waite (right), the Middle East envoy for the Church of England, helped to negotiate Jenco's release. Waite himself was kidnapped by Hezbollah in January 1987 and not released until November 1991.

Lebanon. Between 1984 and 1989, Hezbollah was involved in abducting approximately 70 people in Beirut. Victims included Americans, French, Italians, Germans, Swiss, Russians, Britons, and an Irishman. Some of the hostages were killed, while others died in captivity. One was William F. Buckley, the American in charge of the Central Intelligence Agency (CIA) station in Lebanon. Buckley was abducted on March 15, 1984, and spent 15 months being tortured by Hezbollah terrorists until his death. Other high-profile hostages included journalist Terry Anderson, the Middle East correspondent for the Associated Press, and Terry Waite, an Anglican minister who was in

Lebanon negotiating with Hezbollah for the release of hostages when he was taken prisoner. Both Anderson and Waite were finally released in 1991.

In June of 1985, two Hezbollah terrorists hijacked TWA Flight 847, which was flying from Athens to Rome with more than 150 passengers and crew. The hijackers killed one American, a U.S. Navy sailor named Robert Stethem, and threw his body onto the runway at Beirut, where they had diverted the airliner. The rest of the hostages were eventually freed, in exchange for Israel releasing about 700 Shiite prisoners it had taken in southern Lebanon.

By 1985, the Israelis were holding just a security zone in southern Lebanon. Hezbollah continued its guerrilla attacks, using the ancient city of Baalbek in the Beqaa Valley as a base. The terrorists did not just attack Israeli military targets in Lebanon, they also launched rockets and mortars across the border at Israeli cities. This low-grade conflict continued through the 1990s. Hezbollah terrorists even expanded their reach to hit targets outside of the Middle East. In 1992, the group bombed the Israeli Embassy in Buenos Aires, Argentina, killing 29 people. Two years later, a bomb at a Jewish community center in Buenos Aires killed 85 people.

Hezbollah was popular in Lebanon because of its successful attacks against

Israel, but the group also gained public support by developing a system of social programs intended to help poor Shiite Muslims. The group developed a political wing to provide the sort of services that Lebanon's government would not provide in southern Lebanon: collecting garbage, providing water, repairing and maintaining roads, and operating schools and hospitals. Hezbollah has its own press agency and operates television and radio stations.

In 1990, the Lebanese civil war ended with the signing of a peace agreement among the various parties. Although this agreement called for all militias to be disarmed, Hezbollah was allowed to keep its weapons and maintain its operations in southern Lebanon.

In 1992 Hasan Nasrallah took over as Hezbollah's leader after Israel assassinated the previous leader, Abbas al-

The flag of Hezbollah.

Musawi. That year, for the first time the political wing of Hezbollah fielded candidates for the legislative elections in Lebanon. The party won 12 of the 128 seats in the country's parliament in 1992. Over the next decade, the group would slowly increase its representation in municipal governments as well.

In 2000 Israel withdrew its military

A Shiite woman holds a picture of Hezbollah leader Hasan Nasrallah during a 2006 protest march in Beirut. Nasrallah has been in charge of the organization since 1992, when he succeeded Abbas al-Musawi.

forces from southern Lebanon. Hezbollah guerrillas quickly moved to seize control over all of southern Lebanon, and violence broke out between Lebanese Christians and Muslims. The United Nations sent peacekeepers into the region to end the fighting. Throughout the Arab world, Nasrallah was cheered as a hero whose forces had defeated Israel.

Although the United Nations certified that Israel had left Lebanese territory, Hezbollah continued to attack Israel. It claimed that a small area of land that Israel still occupied known as

Shebaa Farms, which most international authorities recognized as part of Syria, was actually Lebanese territory. The continuing raids, rocket attacks, and terrorist bombings finally led, in the summer of 2006, to a major Israeli attack on Hezbollah facilities in Lebanon. The conflict lasted for more than a month. The army of Lebanon stayed out of the conflict. By the time the Israel-Hezbollah War ended in August 2006, more than 1,300 Lebanese were dead, approximately a million more were refugees, and the infrastructure of southern Lebanon had

Buildings in Beirut damaged by Israeli airstrikes during the 2006 Israel-Hezbollah War. Today Hezbollah controls a stronger militia than the Lebanese army.

Mohammad Fneish (right), pictured here with UN Secretary-General Ban-Ki Moon, is one of two Hezbollah party members to hold a high-ranking position in the government of Lebanon. Fneish is in charge of an agency concerned with reforming the government. Hezbollah's other member of Lebanon's cabinet is Hussein al Hajj Hassan, the minister of agriculture.

been nearly destroyed. Despite this, Hasan Nasrallah claimed at a rally in September that Hezbollah had won a "strategic, historic, and divine victory."

Hezbollah today is a key member of Lebanon's government. It holds a dozen seats in the national legislature and is allied with the Free Patriotic Movement, Lebanon's largest Christian political party. Two Hezbollah party members are in charge of government ministries. However, the group is still considered to be a terrorist organiza-tion. It is known to have a large arsenal of weapons, including an estimated 15,000 short-range rockets, and is sus-pected by some to have been involved in several terrorist attacks in recent years, including the 2005 assassination of prime minister Rafic Hariri and a 2011 bombing in Istanbul, Turkey, that left eight people injured. Although the group has never taken credit for these attacks, it remains viewed with suspi-cion and mistrust by by the United States and many European countries.

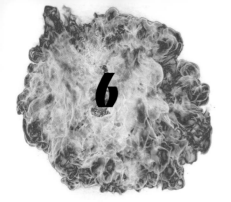

6

THE IRISH REPUBLICAN ARMY

At around 2:10 P.M. on Friday, July 21, 1972, a bomb exploded at a bus station in downtown Belfast. Explosions were nothing new to this city in Northern Ireland, which had been the site of violence between police and anti-government factions for half a dozen years. However, this first bomb was followed a few minutes later by another explosion, then another, and then another. In less than two hours, 22 bombs exploded in Belfast, killing nine people and injuring more than 100.

A group called the Irish Republican Army (IRA) was responsible for this terrorist attack. The incident that became known as "Bloody Friday" was one of more than 1,300 IRA bombings during 1972, the deadliest year in an unsettled period of Irish history known as "the Troubles."

The history of the Irish Republican Army began in 1919, when a rebellion broke out in Ireland against British rule. Ireland had been controlled by the British for centuries, and in 1801 the island had been made part of the United Kingdom, along with England, Scotland, and Wales. Most of the Irish did not like being controlled by the British. A majority of the island's residents were Roman Catholics, who in the British Empire did not enjoy the same rights as other citizens. Several uprisings occurred during the 19th and early 20th centuries before the 1919–1921 conflict known as the Irish War of Independence.

The faction that fought the British were known as "nationalists" (because they wanted to establish Ireland as an independent nation) or "republicans" (because they wanted to set up a republican form of government on the island). The leader of the nationalists' armed wing, called the Irish Republican Army, was a charismatic and brilliant strategist named Michael Collins. Under Collins, the IRA used guerrilla tactics, such as bombings and assassinations, against British troops and against the Royal Irish Constabulary, a police force made up predominantly of Irishmen who were loyal to the United Kingdom. Members of the IRA often conducted hit-and-run raids against police stations, military barracks, and government offices.

The British responded to IRA attacks with harsh reprisals. When British soldiers were wounded or killed, the military would burn the homes and businesses of Irish civilians in retaliation. They also arrested and executed those suspected of aiding the IRA.

The brutal British response helped to turn public opinion among the Irish firmly against continued British rule. By 1921 most of the Irish supported the nationalists. However, in Ulster and six other counties in the northeastern part of the island where the British had a strong industrial presence, a majority of the people wanted to remain part of the United Kingdom. These people were called "unionists."

The war ended when nationalists signed a treaty with the British government. This established the Irish Free State in 1922 as a dominion of the United Kingdom. Dominion status represented a step toward full independence for Ireland. The people of Ireland were given the authority to govern

The seven northernmost counties on the island of Ireland are politically tied to the United Kingdom.

affairs on the island. However, the Irish Free State was still part of the British Empire, which would be responsible for defending the island and conducting foreign affairs on Ireland's behalf.

The dominion arrangement permitted Irish counties to choose whether they wanted to become part of the Irish Free State, or to remain part of the United Kingdom on the same terms as in the past. A day after the Irish Free State was declared, the seven counties in the northern part of the island exercised this right. These counties became known as Northern Ireland, and continued to be ruled from London, while the island's remaining 26 counties made up the Irish Free State and were governed by an Irish parliament in Dublin.

The Irish Free State was soon torn by civil war between a moderate faction called Staters, including Collins, who accepted dominion status and a radical faction, the Republicans, who felt Ireland should gain full independence immediately. Members of the IRA that backed Collins became part of the national army of the Irish Free State. Most members of the IRA supported the Republicans, though.

The civil war cost more lives than the Irish War for Independence had. As in that conflict, both sides used terrorism as a tactic and committed atrocities against civilians in the Free State. The Republicans believed all Ireland should be united under a single Irish government, so they conducted attacks against British facilities there as well, hoping to force the British to withdraw. The Irish Republican Army was responsible for numerous bombings, raids, and street battles both in the Irish Free State and in Northern Ireland. Despite this, supporters of the Irish Free State gradually gained the upper hand. The conflict ended by 1926.

After this, the strength and popularity of the IRA declined. In 1932, Eamon De Valera, a former Republican leader and IRA supporter, was elected to lead the government of the Irish Free State.

However, De Valera soon outlawed the IRA. The organization was also outlawed in Northern Ireland.

Under De Valera, the Irish Free State gained full independence from Great Britain in 1949. In the meantime, Northern Ireland remained part of the United Kingdom. During the 1950s and 1960s, the IRA was a small, secretive organization with few active members. In Northern Ireland, members of the IRA saw their mission as defending nationalists, most of whom were Roman Catholics, from oppression by the unionists who held power, most of whom were Protestants. The IRA occasionally launched attacks against military or police facilities along the border of Northern Ireland.

By the mid-1960s, tensions were rising in Northern Ireland. For decades Roman Catholics in Northern Ireland had been discriminated against when it came to jobs and housing. Many were not permitted to vote. In 1968 Northern Irish Catholics began holding marches and rallies demanding equality. They were inspired by the Civil Rights Movement among African Americans in the United States. In response, Protestants formed paramilitary groups like the Ulster Volunteer Force (UVF), and began to attack the rallies. Riots often followed, with rock-throwing Catholics opposed by police with tear gas, machine guns, and armored cars.

In August 1969, riots broke out in the cities of Belfast, Londonderry, Newry, Strabane, and elsewhere in Northern Ireland. The rioting lasted for five days, with British soldiers finally sent to Northern Ireland to restore order. By the time the riots ended, eight people (6 Catholics, 2 Protestants) were dead and more than 750 were injured. Despite efforts by the IRA to defend Catholic neighborhoods, hundreds of homes and businesses owned by Catholics had been burned down.

As the situation in Northern Ireland deteriorated, the IRA faced an internal conflict. In 1969 the organization split into two wings. One group, calling itself the "official IRA," wanted to establish a communist state in Ireland. Due to lack of support, this faction withered away in the early 1970s. The other, larger, group became known as the "provisional IRA."

Its leaders believed that terrorism against unionists, in addition to attacks on military targets, would drive the British out of Northern Ireland. This marked the start of the Troubles.

The provisional IRA started a terrorist campaign in Northern Ireland. It attacked British army patrols, police stations, and Protestant-owned factories and businesses. Bombings and assassinations were common. Neighborhoods in Belfast and other major cities came to resemble war zones, as IRA members (now sometimes called "Provos") became involved in gun battles with the Ulster Volunteer Force, the Ulster Defense Association, and other Protestant paramilitary groups.

Catholics in Northern Ireland initially welcomed the intervention of the British army, which they thought would protect civilians on both sides. However, the heavy-handed response of

A street in Londonderry, Northern Ireland, devastated by an IRA bomb in July 1972. That year would be the deadliest of the Troubles, with nearly 500 people killed in violence related to the Northern Ireland conflict. In all, between 1969 and 2001, more than 3,500 people would be killed and over 105,000 injured due to the Troubles.

the British soon drove formerly unionist Catholics to the nationalist side. One of the worst incidents occurred on "Bloody Sunday," January 30, 1972, when British paratroopers opened fire on unarmed Catholic demonstrators in Londonderry. Thirteen were killed and 14 others were wounded.

The IRA responded seven months later with the "Bloody Friday" bombings in Belfast. The group also extended its terrorist activities to English soil. In February 1972, an IRA bomb exploded outside the paratroopers' headquarters in Aldershot, England, killing seven people and injuring 18. The next year, IRA car bombs killed one person and injured more than 180 in London. In October and November of 1974, a series of bombs in public restaurants killed 28 people and injured more than 200.

The British government soon passed new anti-terrorism legislation, allowing police to detain suspected Provos without formally charging them with crimes. The legislation, and an increased effort by British authorities to stop paramilitary activities on both sides of the conflict, led to a brief cease-fire in 1975.

The cease fire ended in 1976. That year became the second-deadliest of the Troubles, with 307 people killed—220 of them civilians—as the Provos resumed their campaign of terrorism. To make it harder for British police to infiltrate the IRA, the group was organized into cells.

This way, arrests of a cell would not compromise the activities of other groups.

On August 27, 1979, an IRA cell assassinated Lord Louis Mountbatten, who was a cousin of England's Queen Elizabeth and a respected British statesman. Mountbatten had been vacationing with his family in County Sligo, Ireland. A few hours later bombs set by another IRA cell killed 18 British soldiers in Warrenpoint, Northern Ireland.

During the 1980s, the IRA continued its terrorist activities. In October 1984, the organization detonated a bomb at the Brighton Hotel in England that killed five people and wounded 31. The target had been British Prime Minister Margaret Thatcher, who was staying at the hotel, but she escaped unharmed. The IRA's attacks drew international condemnation. So did the fact that in the mid-1980s Libya provided the organization with thousands of AK-47 machine guns, as well as tons of plastic explosive for bombs.

By the late 1980s it was clear that the IRA would not be able to accomplish its aims only through terrorism. The police of Northern Ireland and British special forces had infiltrated the organization, leading to many arrests. It is estimated that by 1989 about 90 percent of planned IRA attacks were broken up before they could be carried out, or failed to cause casualties.

At the same time, a growing number

of Irish nationalists had begun to work for their goals through elections rather than through violence. Candidates of the political party Sinn Féin, which had long been linked to the IRA, began to win seats in the assembly of Northern Ireland. Gerry Adams, the head of Sinn Féin, was elected in 1983 to represent West Belfast in the parliament of the United Kingdom. (Adams allegedly was a high-ranking member of the IRA at the time, although he has denied this allegation.)

By the early 1990s, the British government was actively trying to end the fighting in Northern Ireland. Hopes for peace were raised in 1994 when the IRA agreed to a cease-fire. Adams and Sinn Féin participated in peace talks with Britain, but in 1996 the IRA resumed its terrorist campaign and the party was barred from the negotiations. In July 1997, the IRA announced a new cease-fire, and Sinn Féin was permitted to rejoin the peace talks.

In April 1998, the Good Friday Agreement was signed. This provided for a new Northern Ireland Assembly comprised of Protestants and Catholics, and greater cooperation between Northern Ireland and the Irish Republic. One condition of the Good

Gerry Adams

Friday Agreement was that all paramilitary groups in Northern Ireland were expected to disarm. The IRA initially refused to comply, delaying full implementation of the agreement, although representatives of Sinn Féin participated in the new Northern Irish government that came into being in December 1999.

By October 2001 the IRA had begun to disarm, and in 2005 the organization announced that it was ending its armed campaign. By July 2006, the British and Irish governments had certified that the IRA had ceased paramilitary and criminal operations.

Sadly, this would not be the last the world would hear of the IRA. In April 2011, a new Irish nationalist terrorist group, largely formed of former Provos, set off a car bomb that killed a young Catholic policeman in Northern Ireland. In a statement taking credit for the murder, the group declared, "Irish republicans have continued to organise against the British presence in our country. We continue to do so under the name of the Irish Republican Army. We are the IRA." This attack seemed to indicate that the terrorist legacy of the Irish Republican Army remains alive and well.

TED KACZYNSKI
THE UNABOMBER

On December 11, 1985, Hugh Scrutton noticed something unusual in the parking lot of the computer store that he owned in Sacramento, California. It appeared to be a block of wood with nails sticking out of it. Scrutton picked up the strange item, probably intending to throw it away before a customer ran over it and damaged his tires. But the moment the block moved, a powerful explosion ripped through the parking lot. The wooden block had contained a powerful bomb packed with metal pieces that would become deadly shrapnel when it exploded. The blast sent dozens of pieces of sharp metal into Scrutton's body, killing the store owner almost immediately.

Investigators soon determined that this bomb was the work of a criminal they had been hunting for many years. He had previously sent bombs through the mail to university professors, and planted one on an airliner. Authorities had nicknamed this unknown criminal the Unabomber, because the FBI name for its investigation into the crimes was "University and Airline Bomber," or UNABOM for short. Several people had been badly hurt by the Unabomber's packages, but Scrutton was the first person killed by one of his bombs.

The Unabomber's first attack had occurred on May 25, 1978. A package supposed to have been mailed by Buckley Crist, an engineering professor at Northwestern University in Illinois, was returned to the professor by the U.S. Postal Service. Crist had not mailed the package, so he asked the university's security guards to examine it. When they did, the bomb inside exploded, injuring a guard. Fortunately, the bomb was amateurish and crude, so it was not very powerful.

A year later, the Unabomber's second bomb exploded at Northwestern University. Again, no one was badly hurt. Six months after that incident, on November 15, 1979, a bomb in the cargo hold of American Airlines Flight 444 began emitting green smoke. The plane made an emergency landing and a dozen passengers were treated for smoke inhalation from the smoldering bomb. They were lucky. If the bomb had exploded, it could have destroyed the aircraft.

Over the next two years, additional bombs were sent. One went to the president of United Airlines. Others went to the University of Utah, Vanderbilt University, and the University of California at Berkeley. The FBI and other agencies investigated the crimes, but had few leads. To throw police investigators off, the Unabomber often included false clues in his bombs. Frustrated, the FBI offered a $1 million reward for information that would lead to the Unabomber's capture.

The bombings stopped for about three years. They restarted again in 1985—only now, the bombs were more powerful. On May 15, 1985, a graduate student at the University of California at Berkeley named John Hauser suffered serious damage to his hand, arm, and eye. Another bomb was found and defused without harming anyone at Auburn University in Washington on June 13. On November 15, Professor

CASE FILE

Name: Theodore John "Ted" Kaczynski

Alias: the Unabomber

Born: May 22, 1942

Location of Terrorist Attacks: Illinois, Utah, Tennessee, California, Washington, Michigan, Connecticut, New Jersey.

Number of victims: 3 killed, 23 injured

Modus Operandi: homemade bombs, often sent through the mail.

Captured: April 3, 1996

Justice: Convicted of all charges and sentences to life imprisonment with no chance of parole.

James V. McConnell and student Nicklaus Suino were injured in an explosion at the University of Michigan. And in December came the bomb that killed Hugh Scrutton in California.

Inspectors believed that during the three-year break, the Unabomber had learned how to make his bombs more effective. These four blasts involved stronger explosives. They were packed with bits of lead, nails, razor blades, and tacks that would become shrapnel and cause greater damage when the bombs exploded. He even "signed" his work, stamping the initials FC into one end of each pipe bomb. Another curious thing was that the bombs were often placed in wooden boxes.

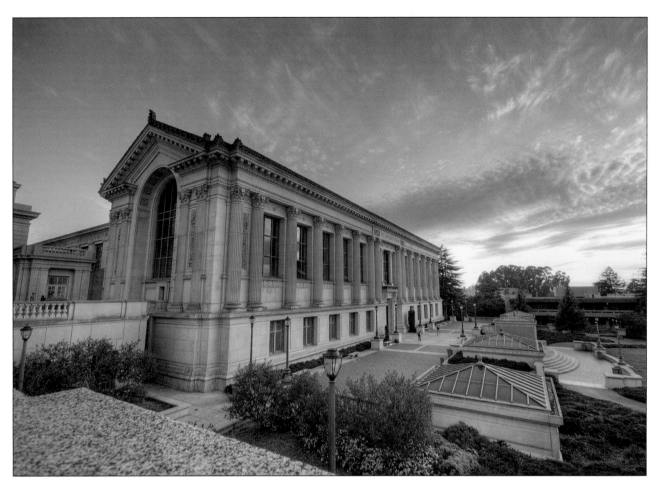

A number of the Unabomber's earliest explosive devices were mailed to professors at the University of California at Berkeley.

In February 1987, the Unabomber struck again. This time, his bomb injured Gary Wright, a computer store owner in Salt Lake City, Utah. However, this time a secretary in a nearby building had seen a man in a hooded sweatshirt and sunglasses placing the bomb in the parking lot of Wright's store. She described the man to the FBI, and a sketch of the suspect was produced and circulated nationally.

For more than six years, there were no new attacks. Police felt that perhaps being seen had scared the Unabomber. But their hope that he had stopped for good ended in June 1993, when two new bombs exploded. These were even more sophisticated than his previous devices had been. They caused serious injury to two professors, Charles Epstein of the University of California and David Gelernter of Yale University.

At the same time, the Unabomber sent a letter to the *New York Times*. He claimed that the attacks were the work of an anarchist group called FC. (The

Unabomber would later write that FC stood for "Freedom Club.") In his letter, the Unabomber said that FC would provide information about its goals "at some future time."

Until this point, several government agencies had each been investigating the Unabomber independently. In 1994 the FBI, the U.S. Postal Service, and the Bureau of Alcohol, Tobacco, and Firearms (ATF) developed a task force devoted to finding the Unabomber. The task force soon grew to more than 150 people working full-time on the case. However, the Unabomber had been very careful when he built his bombs. He often used scrap material that could be found in any garbage dump. And there was no apparent connection between the victims. Investigators would later learn that they had been chosen randomly.

On December 10, 1994, an advertising executive named Thomas Mosser opened a package at his home. It turned out to contain the Unabomber's most powerful device yet. The blast killed Mosser.

On April 20, 1995, perhaps inspired by another act of domestic terrorism, the bombing of a federal office building in Oklahoma City a day earlier, the Unabomber mailed a bomb and several letters. The bomb killed Gilbert Murray, the head of the California Forestry Association. In one of the letters, sent to the *New York Times*, the Unabomber explained his reason for targeting certain people:

> "We blew up Thomas Mosser last December because he was a Burson-Marsteller executive. . . . Burson-Marsteller is about the biggest organization in the public relations field. This means that its business is the development of techniques for manipulating people's attitudes. . . .
>
> "Some news reports have made the misleading statement that we have been attacking universities or scholars. We have nothing against universities or scholars as such. All the university people whom we have attacked have been specialists in technical fields. . . . The people we are out to get are the scientists and engineers, especially in critical fields like computers and genetics. . . . Through our bombings we hope to promote instability in industrial society, propagate anti-industrial ideas and give encouragement to those who hate the industrial system."

In this letter, the Unabomber offered to end his campaign of terrorism if a long essay that he had written was published in a nationally circulated newspaper or magazine. The 35,000-word essay was titled "Industrial Society and

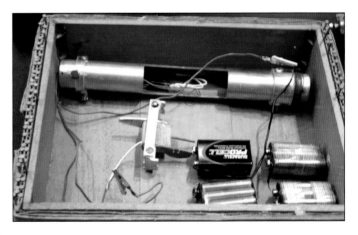

An FBI reproduction of one of the Unabomber's homemade bombs.

The Unabomber was concerned about the effect modern technology, such as computers, would have on society. He used this manual typewriter to produce the letters he sent to authorities, as well as his lengthy manifesto.

its Future," but became commonly known as the "Unabomber Manifesto." In September 1995, the *New York Times* and *Washington Post* printed the manifesto, in which the Unabomber argued that technology and industry were harmful and should be abandoned.

The UNABOM task force had encouraged the newspapers to publish the manifesto in hopes that a reader might be able to identify the author. Thousands of possible suspects were suggested, but one name soon stood out: Ted Kaczynski, a former college professor who was living in a small cabin in rural Montana. His brother David, who had tipped off the FBI, provided letters and documents written by Ted Kaczynski. Based on Kaczynski's writing style, FBI analysts determined

that he had probably written the Unabomber Manifesto.

Ted Kaczynski, born in 1942, had been a mathematics genius, skipping several grades in school and earning a scholarship to Harvard University at age 16. After graduating with a Ph.D. from the University of Michigan, he became a professor at the University of California at Berkeley in 1967, when he was just 25 years old. Although many of his colleagues considered Kaczynski to be brilliant, he suffered from social and emotional problems. In 1969 he suddenly quit his job at Berkeley.

Disillusioned with the world around him, Kaczynski eventually moved to a small cabin that he built in the wilderness near Lincoln, Montana. Kaczynski wanted nothing to do with modern tech-

Ted Kaczynski (left) with his father and brother David in a photo taken during the late 1960s.

nology. His cabin had no electricity or running water. People in Lincoln knew him as "The Hermit." Kaczynski sometimes worked at odd jobs to earn money, but for the most part, he lived off food that he grew or caught.

On April 3, 1996, Ted Kaczynski was arrested. In his cabin, investigators found the parts to build bombs, journals in which he had described Unabomber attacks, and an original copy of the Unabomber Manifesto. They also found a live bomb, ready to be mailed. Despite his promise to stop his attacks if the newspapers printed his manifesto, the Unabomber apparently was not ready to give up terrorism.

After 18 years and 16 bombs that killed three people and inured 23, Ted Kaczynski's reign of terror was finally over. He eventually pled guilty to mailing bombs and to murder charges, and was sentenced to life imprisonment without the possibility of parole.

In the spring of 2011, the Unabomber was back in the news. In May and June, Kaczynski's personal items and writings were sold in an internet auction. The auction raised more than $230,000, which was distributed

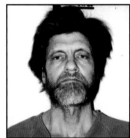

(Top) Ted Kaczynski retreated from the world in this small cabin in rural Montana that he had built himself during the 1970s. (Right) Booking photo of the Unabomber taken after his arrest in April 1996.

to the victims of his attacks. Around the same time, federal authorities sought a sample of Kaczynski's DNA, as they suspected he might have been involved in the 1982 poisoning of Tylenol pain medication that had killed seven people and caused a national panic. However, investigators could not prove a link between Kaczynski and the poisonings.

Kaczynski is currently incarcerated at the high-security Florence ADX penitentiary in Colorado.

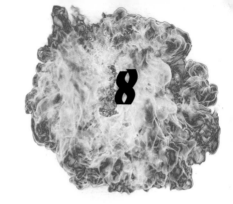

8

Investigators search through the rubble of the Alfred P. Murrah Building in Oklahoma City. Half of the building collapsed after a powerful explosion in April 1995. The terrorist attack killed 168 people and shocked the nation.

TIMOTHY MCVEIGH
OKLAHOMA CITY BOMBER

At a few minutes after 9 A.M. on the morning of April 19, 1995, an enormous explosion rocked Oklahoma City. When the smoke cleared, a U.S. government office building was in ruins, 168 people were dead, and more than 500 others were injured.

The attack was obviously an act of terrorism, and investigators initially believed that a radical Muslim or Middle Eastern group was probably responsible. However, they soon determined that the bombing had not been committed by a foreign enemy. Instead, an American citizen had detonated a bomb outside the building as a protest against what he considered to be the U.S. government's tyranny against its own citizens.

The "homegrown terrorist," Timothy McVeigh, had been born in upstate New York in 1968. His parents divorced when he was ten. As a young man,

McVeigh was interested in computers and guns.

After graduating from high school, McVeigh briefly went to college, then enlisted in the U.S. Army. During basic training in 1988, McVeigh met Terry Nichols. Although Nichols was 13 years older than McVeigh, the two became good friends. Another of McVeigh's friends was Michael Fortier, who was stationed at Fort Riley, Kansas, with Nichols and McVeigh during the late 1980s.

McVeigh served in the 1991 Gulf War, and received the Bronze Star for his heroism. After returning from Iraq, McVeigh left the military. He seemed unable to settle down, quitting several jobs and spending time driving across the country visiting old army friends. McVeigh spoke with them about how disillusioned he had become about the U.S. government, which he believed robbed people of their freedom through taxes and regulatory laws.

One of the friends McVeigh visited with during this period was Terry Nichols, who had left the army in 1989. The two men worked together selling weapons at gun shows in the early 1990s. Nichols shared McVeigh's negative feelings about the government. He attended meetings of anti-government groups and tried to renounce his U.S. citizenship, claiming that the government had no jurisdiction over him.

In the early 1990s, a series of violent encounters between federal agents and other anti-government dissidents angered both Nichols and McVeigh. In 1992, FBI agents and federal marshals attempted to arrest a man named Randy Weaver at his rural cabin in Ruby Ridge, Idaho. During an 11-day standoff, Weaver's wife and son were shot and killed by FBI snipers. Another incident occurred the next year, when agents of the FBI and the U.S. Bureau of Alcohol, Tobacco and Firearms (ATF) surrounded a compound occupied by a religious group called the Branch Davidians in Waco, Texas. The 51-day siege ended on April 19, 1993, when the FBI agents

The Branch Davidian compound near Waco, Texas, is engulfed by flames after a raid by federal authorities on April 19, 1993.

attacked the compound, shooting at the cult's members. The Branch Davidian compound was destroyed by a fire and 76 members of the group, including its leader David Koresh, were killed.

During the Waco siege, McVeigh visited the town to pass out anti-government pamphlets and show support for the Branch Davidians. However, he was with Terry Nichols at Nichols's brother's farm in Michigan when the Waco siege ended in fiery disaster. The two men soon began to plan an attack on the U.S. government.

During the next year, McVeigh and Nichols bought—and sometimes stole— the components they would need to make a powerful bomb. They stored some of the material at their friend Michael Fortier's home in Arizona, where McVeigh could practice making and detonating homemade bombs in the nearby desert without fear of being bothered by authorities. Other weapons and bomb material was stored near a house Nichols bought in Kansas.

By September of 1994, McVeigh had selected the target for his attack—the Alfred P. Murrah Federal Building in Oklahoma City. The building held local offices for a number of government agencies, including the ATF, the Drug Enforcement Administration (DEA), the U.S. Secret Service, the Social Security Administration, and the Department of Housing and Urban

CASE FILE

Name: Timothy James McVeigh
Born: April 23, 1968
Location of Attack: Oklahoma City
Number of victims: 168 killed, more than 500 injured
Modus Operandi: truck bomb
Captured: April 19, 1995
Justice: Convicted in 1997 and sentenced to death; executed by lethal injection on June 11, 2001

Development (HUD). It also contained recruiting offices for the army and the U.S. Marine Corps. Altogether, more than 500 people worked in the Murrah building. It apparently didn't bother McVeigh that most of them were civilians working for the government, or that there was a day care facility for children located inside the Murrah building. He believed destroying this building would make a strong political statement about what he considered the government's growing infringement on the rights of Americans.

McVeigh would later write a letter explaining that, from his perspective, the bombing of the Murrah building was simply a counterattack in an ongoing conflict between the U.S. government and its own citizens:

> Foremost, the bombing was a retaliatory strike: a counter-attack, for the cumulative raids (and subsequent violence and damage) that federal agents had participated in over the preceding years (including, but not limited to, Waco). From the formation of such units as the FBI's "Hostage Rescue" and other assault teams amongst federal agencies during the 80s, culminating in the Waco incident, federal actions grew increasingly militaristic and violent, to the point where at Waco, our government—like the Chinese—was deploying tanks against its own citizens. . . .
>
> Therefore, this bombing was also meant as a pre-emptive (or pro-active) strike against those forces and their command and control centers within the federal building. When an aggressor force continually launches attacks from a particular base of operations, it is sound military strategy to take the fight to the enemy. Additionally, borrowing a page from U.S. foreign policy, I decided to send a message to a government that was becoming increasingly hostile, by bombing a government building and the government employees within that building who represent that government.

By April 1995, McVeigh was ready to proceed with the plan. On April 15, he rented a yellow Ryder truck from a Kansas agency, and the next day McVeigh and Nichols drove to Oklahoma City, where they left a getaway car a few blocks away from the Murrah building. On April 17-18, they constructed a powerful bomb in the back of the rental truck. The bomb consisted of about 5,000 pounds of volatile agricultural fertilizer, diesel fuel, and other explosive chemicals. McVeigh planned to detonate this bomb the next day, April 19, because that was the day the Branch Davidian compound in Waco had been destroyed by federal agents two years earlier.

Nichols drove back home, while McVeigh slept in the Ryder truck that night. Early the next morning, McVeigh drove the truck to Oklahoma City, arriving at the Murrah building shortly before 9 A.M. He parked the truck in front of the building, ignited two fuses that would detonate the bomb, then quickly walked toward his getaway car.

The truck bomb exploded at 9:02 A.M. with devastating force. It destroyed one-third of the building, creating a crater eight feet deep and 20 feet across that was filled with rubble. The blast damaged several other buildings nearby. The shock wave from the explosion knocked people in offices several blocks away out of their chairs. A psychologist who was working about 20 blocks away said the blast "shook the daylights out of things—it scared us to death. We felt the windows shake before we heard the noise."

A rescue operation soon began, with firefighters and police trying to pull people from the rubble. It was slow, dangerous work, as the badly damaged building looked like it could collapse completely at any time. Eventually it was determined that the explosion had killed 168 people—19 of them children—and injured hundreds more.

Just 90 minutes after the bombing, while the rescue operation was still underway, Timothy McVeigh was arrested. He was driving back to Kansas when he was pulled over by an Oklahoma state police trooper because his car did not have a license plate. When the trooper found that McVeigh was carrying an unlicensed handgun, he arrested him. At the time, no one realized that McVeigh was the Oklahoma City bomber. McVeigh was held in the jail in Perry, Oklahoma, to await a hearing on the gun charges.

In the meantime, the FBI and other agencies were conducting a national manhunt for the bomber. At first they suspected Muslim terrorists, such as the ones who had carried out the 1993 World Trade Center bombing. However, agents were able to identify the Ryder truck from a serial number printed on its axle. They traced the vehicle to the Kansas agency that had rented the truck to McVeigh. The owner of the agency was able to describe the man who had rented the truck; a sketch based on his description bore a strong resemblance to McVeigh. The FBI was shocked to learn that McVeigh was already in

CASE FILE

Name: Terry Lynn Nichols

Born: April 1, 1955

Location of Attack: Oklahoma City

Number of victims: 168 killed, more than 500 injured

Role in attack: Helped Timothy McVeigh to construct truck bomb and attempt getaway

Captured: April 21, 1995

Justice: Convicted of killing eight federal law enforcement officers in 1998; in 2000, convicted of 161 additional murder charges in Oklahoma state court. Currently serving sentence of life imprisonment with no possibility of parole

prison in Perry. On April 21, immediately after McVeigh's hearing on the gun charges, federal agents took him into their custody as a suspect in the Oklahoma City bombing.

That same day, Terry Nichols turned himself in to the authorities. A search of

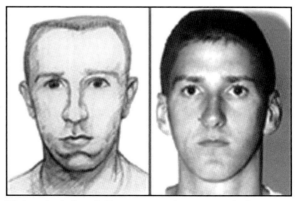

This sketch of the man who rented the truck used in the bombing bore a strong resemblance to Timothy McVeigh.

Federal agents take Timothy McVeigh into custody, April 1995.

his home turned up material used to make the bomb, as well as other evidence that linked both him and McVeigh to the crime.

Michael Fortier and his wife Lori were also arrested. Although Michael Fortier had refused to help McVeigh carry out the actual bombing, he had been involved in the planning, while Lori Fortier had made a fake drivers license for McVeigh that he used to rent the Ryder truck. They agreed to testify against McVeigh and Nichols in exchange for reduced sentences.

The trial of Timothy McVeigh began in January 1996 and lasted for more than a year. On June 2, 1997, a jury found McVeigh

Terry Nichols

guilty and he was sentenced to be executed. McVeigh did not speak in his own defense during the trial. After his sentencing, McVeigh never expressed any remorse over killing civilians with the bombing. He claimed that he had carried out the attack on the Murrah building without help from anyone else.

The trial of Terry Nichols began in November 1998. Despite McVeigh's claim that he had worked alone, the Fortiers and more than 100 other people testified that Nichols had been involved in the plot. On December 23, 1998, Nichols was convicted for his role in the bombing and sentenced to life in prison without the possibility of parole. He is currently housed in a cell at the ADX

On April 19, 2000, the Oklahoma City National Memorial was dedicated at the former site of the Murrah building. The 168 empty chairs each represent a victim of the terrorist attack.

Florence maximum security federal prison in Colorado. Because terrorists Ramzi Yousef and Ted Kaczynski are also imprisoned in the same cell block of that prison, it has been nicknamed "bomber's row."

McVeigh stopped appealing his death sentence, and did little to prevent his execution from taking place. On June 11, 2001—little more than six years after he had killed 168 people in what was the worst terrorist attack on American soil to that point in history—McVeigh was strapped to a table in an Indiana prison. There, officials of the government that McVeigh hated injected lethal chemicals into his bloodstream and he died at 7:14 A.M.

9

PALESTINIAN TERRORIST GROUPS

The establishment of the state of Israel in 1948 would eventually lead to a major increase in the use of terrorism. Palestine, a region on the eastern Mediterranean Sea, had once been the homeland of the Jewish people, but in the second century A.D., Roman troops had forcibly expelled most of the Jews from Palestine. Jews eventually settled in many countries around the world. Because they maintained their religious and cultural traditions, they often became the targets of discrimination, harassment, and even organized massacres by Christian or Muslim majorities in those countries.

By the late 19th century, Jews had begun returning to Palestine, in hopes of re-establishing a homeland where they would be free from persecution. (People who supported the idea of a Jewish homeland in Palestine were called Zionists.) By the time World War

II began in 1939, more than 250,000 Jews had emigrated to Palestine. However, as the Jewish population increased, so did tensions with the native Arabs of Palestine, who resented the newcomers' presence.

The end of World War II in 1945 profoundly changed the situation in Palestine. The Holocaust, the Nazi attempt to exterminate the Jewish population of Europe, had resulted in nearly 6 million deaths. After the war hundreds of thousands of European Jews hoped to emigrate to Palestine. However, the British government, which had ruled the territory since 1917, refused to allow more Jews to emigrate to Palestine.

In an attempt to change the British policy, Jewish paramilitary groups began launching terrorist attacks against railroads, government buildings, British soldiers, and Arab villages. In

(Left) Survivors of the Holocaust wanted to establish a Jewish state in Palestine where they could be safe from future persecution. (Right) David Ben-Gurion declares Israel's independence in Tel Aviv, May 14, 1948. Behind him is a portrait of 19th century Zionist Theodor Herzl.

July 1946 a Zionist group called Irgun bombed the King David Hotel in Jerusalem, where the British maintained a command center. The blast killed more than 90 British, Arabs, and Jews. Palestinian Arabs responded with terrorist tactics by their own militias, while the British attempted to maintain order by stationing more than 100,000 soldiers in the region.

In 1947, Britain asked the newly formed United Nations to help resolve the crisis in Palestine. The U.N. came up with a plan to divide Palestine into two independent states—one Jewish and one Arab. Zionists reluctantly said they would accept the plan, but the Arabs refused the partition of Palestine outright. The fighting between Jews and Arabs escalated.

On May 14, 1948, the British officially withdrew from Palestine, and Zionist leaders proclaimed the independence of the State of Israel. Almost immediately, neighboring Arab states Egypt, Syria, Transjordan (Jordan), Lebanon, and Iraq sent armies to crush the new Jewish state. However, Israeli forces held off the much larger Arab armies. By the time the fighting ended in 1949, Israel controlled about 75 percent of Palestine. The remaining territory was seized by Egypt and Transjordan.

The 1948-49 war was a disaster for the Palestinian Arabs. Hundreds of Arab villages had been destroyed, and approx-

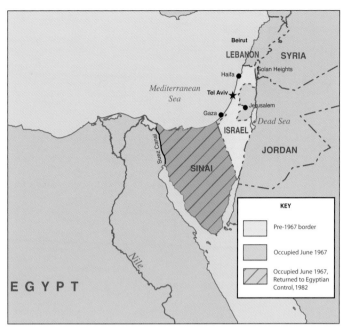

In the June 1967 War, Israel gained control of the West Bank and Gaza Strip, two territories where many Palestinians had been living. The country also seized control of the Sinai Peninsula, although that was later returned to Egypt.

imately 750,000 Palestinians—more than half the total population—had fled to neighboring countries as refugees.

Over the next 18 years, the leaders of Arab countries regularly threatened to invade and destroy Israel. The Palestinian refugees held out hope that they would one day be able to return. But as it became clear that the Arab states were unwilling or unable to back up their threats against Israel with action, some Palestinians began to organize themselves with the goal of "liberating" Palestine from Israeli control. One of these groups was al-Fatah (the Victory Party), which was founded in 1959 by a Palestinian named Yasir Arafat. By the

mid-1960s, al-Fatah was launching guerrilla raids and terrorist attacks inside Israel. In 1964 the Palestine Liberation Organization (PLO) was established to coordinate the activities of Palestinian nationalist groups.

Israel's surprise victory over Egypt, Syria, and Jordan in the June 1967 "Six-Day War" proved that the Palestinians could not count on others to win back the territory they had lost. Arafat and his militant al-Fatah faction soon gained control of the PLO. In 1968 Arafat issued the Palestine National Charter, which said that the Palestinians were entitled to the entire territory and declared, "Armed struggle is the only way to liberate Palestine."

More than a dozen Palestinian paramilitary groups, known as *fedayeen*, launched terrorist attacks against Israeli targets between 1968 and 1970. They set off bombs in public areas, targeting both soldiers and civilians in order to increase public fear. One of these most notorious groups was the Popular Front for the Liberation of Palestine (PFLP), which was founded by George Habash and Wadia Haddad. Others included the Democratic Front for the Liberation of Palestine (DFLP) and the Arab Liberation Front. Arafat's PLO received funds and weapons from Arab countries and distributed them to the *fedayeen*.

Soon, the *fedayeen* began to commit acts of international terrorism in order

Israeli police examine the bodies of Palestinian *fedayeen* killed in a border raid during the 1960s.

to draw attention to the Palestinian cause. In July 1968 the PFLP hijacked an airliner flown by Israel's state-owned airline, El Al. The terrorists ordered the pilot to fly the plane to Algeria, an Arab country in North Africa. There, they held 32 Israeli passengers and crew members for more than a month, until Israel agreed to release a number of Arab prisoners.

This success led to numerous other airline hijackings, or skyjackings. The PFLP did not only target El Al planes. They also skyjacked American and European airliners because their governments supported Israel. The skyjacking crisis peaked in September 1970, when Palestinian terrorists simultaneously captured planes from British Airlines, Pan Am, Swissair, and TWA, and failed in an attempt to take over an

El Al flight. Three of the aircraft were blown up in front of the international media after the passengers had been taken off the planes. The September 1970 skyjackings brought the PFLP worldwide notoriety and thousands of new recruits.

Soon, however, the Palestinians would be involved in a bloody confrontation with the government of Jordan, where most of the terrorist groups were based. Jordan's King Hussein feared that the PFLP and other well-armed Palestinian groups posed a threat to his control over the country. In fact, some Palestinians had been talking about taking over the government, and in early September an attempt to assassinate the king failed.

On September 16, 1970, Jordan's armed forces began attacking camps and bases operated by terrorist groups. After two weeks of attacks during what became known as "Black September," some 3,000 to 5,000 Palestinians had been killed. Ultimately, the Palestinians were forced to move their operations from Jordan to southern Lebanon, near that country's border with Israel.

Despite this, the terrorists continued their attacks. On May 30, 1972, the PFLP teamed up with another terrorist group, the Japanese Red Army, to attack passengers at Lod Airport in Israel. Eight gunmen killed 26 people, including 17 American tourists, and injured nearly 80 others.

An even more notorious attack would occur during the 1972 Summer Olympic Games in Munich, Germany,

A masked Black September terrorist on the balcony of the dormitory where Israel's Olympic team was staying during the Munich games, September 1972. The murder of 11 Israeli athletes shocked the world.

when armed members of a Palestinian group calling itself Black September attempted to kidnap Israeli athletes on September 5. When the crisis ended, the terrorists had killed 11 athletes and a West German policeman. The attack drew worldwide outrage, but also attracted greater attention to the Palestinian cause.

By the mid-1970s, the Palestinian Liberation Organization had begun to gain international legitimacy. In 1974 Yasir Arafat officially declared that the group would no longer commit violent attacks outside of Israel and the territories that it occupied. Later that year the United Nations granted the PLO "observer status," which meant that the organization could participate in some UN activities and discussions as the official representative of the Palestinian people. Arafat became something of a celebrity, regularly traveling to meet with world leaders to discuss the plight of the Palestinian people.

As the PLO attempted to enter the mainstream of international politics, many of the most militant Palestinian groups, including the PFLP, broke away from the organization and continued their violent attacks. Another group that emerged at this time was the Abu Nidal Organization, which committed dozens of attacks that killed hundreds of people during the 1970s and 1980s. Abu Nidal, the organization's leader, was a ruthless terrorist backed by Iraq and Libya.

Arafat's Fatah organization, which remained part of the PLO, also continued to carry out attacks. In March 1978 the group hijacked a bus on the highway near Tel Aviv. They killed 38 Israelis, including 13 children, and wounded 76 other people.

This attack and others would lead Israel to invade southern Lebanon later in 1978, with the goal of moving the Palestinians away from Israel's border. Israel conducted a second invasion of Lebanon in 1982; this time, Arafat and the PLO were forced to relocate to Tunisia. However, the invasions had the unintended consequence of spawning new terrorist groups in Lebanon, such as the Shiite Muslim organization Hezbollah.

The terrorist attacks did little to improve the condition of most Palestinians. In the mid-1980s, the Palestinian refugees were still living in squalid camps in Jordan, Lebanon, Egypt, and other Arab states. They had never been able to assimilate into the Arab societies that hosted them. The number of people living in the camps had grown to more than 2 million. In addition, during the early 1980s Israel had begun building settlements in Palestinian territories that the country had occupied since the June 1967 War. In 1984 Israel began a massive road-

Yasir Arafat speaks at the United Nations, 1974.

building project to connect the West Bank settlements directly to Israel. Many people felt the government's primary goal was to reduce the size of a future Palestinian state.

In 1985, members of the Palestine Liberation Front hijacked an Italian cruise ship, the *Achille Lauro*, demanding the release of 50 prisoners held in Israeli jails. A wheelchair-bound 69-year-old Jewish American man named Leon Klinghoffer was killed and his body thrown overboard by the terrorists. The terrorists eventually gave up the ship in exchange for a promise of safe conduct back to Tunisia. However, the U.S. military intercepted the Egyptian airliner that was carrying the terrorists, forcing it to land in Italy, where the terrorists were arrested.

In another plot later that year, members the Abu Nidal Organization opened fire on people waiting in line at the El Al counters at the Rome and Vienna airports. Nineteen people were killed and more than 140 wounded in these simultaneous attacks.

In late 1987, the growing anger among Palestinians in the Israeli-occupied West Bank and Gaza Strip erupted into a violent uprising. Known as the *intifada* (which in Arabic means "shaking off"), it included many attacks against Israeli settlers and soldiers. Israel responded by sending troops and tanks to maintain order. The uprising attracted international sympathy to the Palestinian cause, as television crews regularly captured views of stone-throwing Palestinian youths being confronted by well-armed Israeli soldiers. The three-year-long *intifada* did not result in Israel withdrawing from the territories. It did however lead to the formation of several new Palestinian groups. One of these was Hamas, which was based in the Gaza Strip.

Unlike the PLO and most other Palestinian terrorist groups, Hamas was established by Islamic fundamentalists. They wanted to create a Palestinian state governed by Islamic law. As a result Hamas found itself not only waging war with Israel, but also fighting against Yasir Arafat and the PLO for control of Palestinians in the Gaza Strip. Hamas had both political and militant wings; the group's paramilitary was known as the al-Qassam Brigades and conducted numerous attacks on Israeli targets. It often worked with another group of Muslim fundamentalists known as Palestinian Islamic Jihad.

By the early 1990s the PLO was

The squalid conditions experienced by Palestinians living in the West Bank and Gaza Strip led in 1987 to an uprising (*intifada*) that lasted for several years.

willing to work with Israel in order to achieve a Palestinian state. In 1993, PLO chairman Yasir Arafat signed an agreement with Israel called the Oslo Accords. Israel agreed to gradually permit limited Palestinian self-government in the occupied territories, and to continue negotiations toward an independent Palestinian state, while the PLO formally recognized the right of Israel to exist and promised to end its terrorist attacks. When the agreement was sealed in September 1993 with an historic handshake between Arafat and Israeli prime minister Yitzhak Rabin on the White House lawn, it seemed that after decades of fighting, the Palestinian crisis might finally be coming to an end.

Ultimately, this was not to be, as neither the PLO (which formed a new governing body called the Palestinian Authority) nor Israel could control extremists who were opposed to the agreement. In 1994 an Israeli named Baruch Goldstein shot and killed 29 unarmed Palestinian Muslims praying at a mosque in the West Bank. The next year, a Jewish extremist named Yigal Amir assassinated prime minister Rabin.

Arafat, meanwhile, could not stop groups like Hamas and Palestinian Islamic Jihad from continuing their violence. These two groups became particularly known for suicide bombings. A terrorist would carry explosives to a designated target, knowing they would die

In September 1993 it seemed the Israeli-Palestinian dispute might end peacefully after an historic agreement between Israel's Prime Minister Yitzhak Rabin and Yasir Arafat's Palestine Liberation Organization. However, the peace process collapsed seven years later.

while taking a large number of people, often civilians, with them. In 1994 a member of Hamas detonated a bomb on a bus in Tel Aviv, killing 22 people (including himself) and injuring 50 more. In 1996 Hamas suicide bombers blew up two buses in Jerusalem, killing 45 people and injuring dozens more. Numerous attacks during the 1990s created fear throughout Israel and poisoned the prospects for peace.

In July of 2000, U.S. President Bill Clinton hosted a meeting between Israeli and Palestinian leaders, hoping to resolve the final issues and establish a Palestinian state. The talks failed, as the two sides could not agree on several

Israelis stand outside an apartment building in Ashkelon that was damaged by a rocket fired from the Gaza Strip.

of the most important issues, including the borders of the new state and the right of Palestinian refugees to return to their former homes in Israel.

In September of 2000, a second Palestinian *intifada* began in the West Bank and Gaza Strip. The number of suicide bombings rose, and soon groups like Hamas began using a new tactic to terrorize the Israeli civilian population. In 2001 they began launching rockets at Israeli settlements in the Gaza Strip, as well as at nearby towns like Sderot. Over the next decade, more than 8,500 rockets would be randomly launched at targets in southern Israel. The attacks killed dozens of people and no one living there could feel completely safe.

The government of Israel responded by restricting Palestinian freedoms and retaliating against suicide attacks with military force. The prospect for peace vanished beneath new waves of terror and repression.

During the summer of 2005, the government of Israel decided to withdraw completely from the Gaza Strip. Settlements were dismantled, and Israeli settlers were forcibly evicted from their homes. Israeli troops left in September 2005, turning control over to the Palestinian Authority and its president, Mahmoud Abbas of Fatah.

Abbas, who had been elected after the death of Arafat in 2004, was no more effective at keeping the hardline terrorists of Hamas and Palestinian Islamic Jihad in line than Arafat had been. In a legislative election held in January 2006, Hamas won a majority of seats and took control over the government of the Gaza Strip. Fighting between supporters of Hamas and Fatah intensified, with both parties claiming to

Israel has responded to Hamas rocket attacks with airstrikes that have destroyed homes, businesses, hospitals, and power stations in Gaza. Here, Palestinians look at damage caused by an Israeli airstrike in November 2012.

be the legitimate voice of the Palestinian people. Also, after the election the United States, European Union, and other countries cut off humanitarian aid that they had been providing to help the Palestinians because of Hamas's terrorist activities. Israel too refused to deal with the Hamas-led government in the Gaza Strip.

Hamas and other groups have continued their rocket attacks and suicide bombings. Israel periodically responds with military force directed at the terrorists. In late 2008, Israel invaded the Gaza Strip with the goal of stopping the rocket attacks. When three weeks of fighting ended in early 2009, more than 1,400 Palestinians had been killed and over 5,500 wounded.

Despite this, the rocket attacks have never been stopped. In March 2012, Hamas members launched more than 300 rockets into southern Israel, wounding 23 civilians. Israel retaliated with air strikes on the Gaza Strip, killing 22 militants. In November 2012, after an Israeli airstrike killed Ahmed Jabari, the second-ranking military commander of Hamas, the group fired more than 1,400 rockets at southern Israel, killing six people and injuring hundreds more.

According to statistics kept by the Israeli Ministry of Foreign Affairs, more than 3,000 civilians and soldiers have been killed in Israel by terrorist attacks since the country was established in 1948. This figure does not include the hundreds more killed outside the country, or the tens of thousands of Palestinians who have been killed in terrorist attacks or Israeli reprisals. Terrorism has not helped the Palestinians, but tragically it continues to be employed in this long-running conflict over an ancient land.

RED ARMY FACTION
THE BAADER-MEINHOF GANG

After the Second World War ended in 1945, the victorious Allied powers—the United States, Great Britain, France, and the Soviet Union—divided defeated Germany into two states. East Germany was a Communist country that fell under Soviet influence. West Germany was aligned with the United States and other democracies.

Konrad Adenauer, the leader of West Germany's government from 1949 until 1963, succeeded in establishing the country as a democracy. He also rebuilt the country's economy, and by the 1960s West Germany was among the most prosperous nations of Europe. Adenauer had strong anti-communist views, and wanted to make sure that West Germany never became part of the Communist bloc of nations. These views were shared by subsequent German chancellors in the 1960s.

Despite West Germany's successful reconstruction from the devastation of World War II, not everyone believed that democracy was the best approach for the country. By the late 1960s, a protest movement had developed among young people in West Germany. These students felt that the German government represented the interests of the wealthy upper classes, rather than their own. The German students were inspired by the writings of Karl Marx and by the revolutionary activities of Mao Zedong, Ho Chi Minh, Che Guevara and other Communists. They were offended by the hypocrisy of former Nazi Party members who had gained powerful positions in West German government and business. (Kurt Georg Kiesinger, chancellor of Germany from 1966 to 1969, had been a member of the Nazi Party in the 1930s and 1940s.) The students also protested against the involvement of West Germany's allies, like the United States, in conflicts against Communist states like Vietnam.

In April of 1968, 25-year-old Andreas Baader, his girlfriend, Gudrun Ensslin, and two other men set fire to two department stores in Frankfurt, West Germany. Their intent was to protest against the Vietnam War. The four were arrested after a few days, convicted, and sentenced to three years in prison.

Baader and Ensslin were paroled in 1969; when government authorities demanded that they return to prison, they fled the country instead. They traveled to France, where they spent time with a left-wing journalist and former associate of Che Guevara's named Régis Debray.

In 1969, while in Italy, Baader and Ensslin met with Horst Mahler, a left-wing activist and lawyer who had defended them during the 1968 trial. Mahler convinced them to return to West Germany and start an underground revolutionary group.

Soon after Baader returned to West Germany, he was arrested at a traffic stop. While he was in prison, Ensslin and Mahler came up with a daring plan to free him. A well-known left-wing journalist named Ulrike Meinhof arranged to meet with Baader to work on a book project. The police gave permission for Meinhof to interview the

CASE FILE

Name: Andreas Bernd Baader

Born: May 6, 1943

Location of Attacks: West Germany

Type of attacks: participated in bombings and armed robberies; founder and leader of the Red Army Faction, which was responsible for hundreds of bombings and 34 deaths.

Captured: June 1, 1972, after a shootout with police

Justice: convicted in April 1977 of murder, attempted murder, and forming a terrorist organization and sentenced to life in prison

Died: October 18, 1977, in prison

prisoner in a Berlin library. Baader was wearing civilian clothes, but escorted by two German police guards. During the interview, two young women, confederates of Meinhof, allowed a masked gunman into the library. They overwhelmed the guards and escaped with Baader through the window. A few weeks later, police received a mocking message announcing the formation of a new organization: the Red Army Faction.

The West German police launched a massive manhunt for Baader, Meinhof, Ensslin, and Mahler, but they escaped from the country. They first went to East Germany, then to Beirut, Lebanon. There, for a few months during 1970 they received training at a camp run by

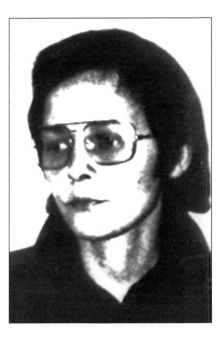

Andreas Baader (left) and his girlfriend Gudrun Ensslin (center) were the leaders of the Red Army Faction. Journalist Ulrike Meinhof's name is incorporated into the name by which this terrorist organization was known in 1970s West Germany (the "Baader-Meinhof gang"), but Meinhof never really had a leadership position in the Red Army Faction.

the terrorist group Popular Front for the Liberation of Palestine.

In August 1970 Baader and his cohorts secretly returned to West Germany. They enticed several dozen young people to join the Red Army Faction, and began robbing banks, using the stolen money to pay for weapons and explosives. The RAF used these to bomb U.S. military facilities in West Germany, as well as police stations, newspaper offices, and other buildings that to the radical group represented the established government. They also attempted to assassinate judges, business leaders, and other high-profile West Germans. By 1972 the group's attacks had killed six people

and injured more than 100. Although the terrorists referred to themselves with the name Red Army Faction, the German media often called the organization the "Baader-Meinhof Gang."

Finally, in June 1972 the West German police captured Baader, Ensslin, Meinhof, and their associates Holger Meins and Jan-Carl Raspe. The terrorists were imprisoned in the high-security Stammheim Prison in Stuttgart.

German officials hoped that the arrests would end the Red Army Faction's campaign of terror. But while Baader and his followers languished in prison, a new generation of radicals continued committing terrorist attacks in the name of the RAF. These included the kidnapping of a German politician, who was later released in exchange for the government freeing some RAF members, and the bombing of the West German embassy in Stockholm, Sweden.

Despite these attacks, the government refused to release Baader and the other high-ranking terrorist leaders. Their trial began in 1975 and lasted for two years. Two of the five RAF leaders died before the trial ended. In 1974, Holger Meins died of starvation; he had been on a hunger strike to protest conditions in the prison. In 1976, Ulrike Meinhof was found dead in her jail cell. She had apparently hanged herself, although RAF sympathizers claimed that she had been murdered by the West German police.

On April 7, 1977, the West German official in charge of prosecuting the Red Army Faction leaders was assassinated, along with his driver and bodyguard. Despite this attack, three weeks later Baader, Ensslin, and Raspe were convicted and sentenced to life imprisonment for their crimes.

The Red Army Faction stepped up its efforts, hoping to secure the terrorists' release. In June 1977 members of the group murdered a banker while trying to kidnap him. In September, a leading German industrialist named Hanns-Martin Schleyer was kidnapped by the RAF, which threatened to kill him unless Baader and the others were released. The West German government refused.

On October 13, 1977, four members of the Popular Front for the Liberation of Palestine hijacked Lufthansa Flight 181. They held 86 passengers and five crew members prisoner, and demanded the release of Baader, Ensslin, Raspe, seven other imprisoned RAF members, two Palestinians jailed in Turkey, and a $15 million ransom. The terrorists eventually directed the plane to Mogadishu, Somalia.

Jan-Carl Raspe

At around 2 A.M. on the morning of October 18, members of a West German anti-terrorism agency called Grenzschutzgruppe 9 (GSG 9) stormed the plane in a surprise attack. They managed to kill three of the terrorists and free the hostages.

Later that morning, when they learned about the failed hijacking, Baader, Ensslin, and Raspe committed suicide in their prison cells. They apparently hoped to become martyrs and draw new radicals to the Red Army Faction. At the same time, the RAF executed their businessman hostage Schleyer.

Despite the deaths of its founders, the Red Army Faction continued to launch terrorist attacks in West

This logo appeared on correspondence from the Red Army Faction, including letters claiming credit for terrorist attacks and essays on the group's ideology written by Horst Mahler and Ulrike Meinhof.

Germany. In 1979, the group attempted to assassinate U.S. General Alexander Haig, who at the time was the commander of NATO. In August and September of 1981 the group launched several attacks against U.S. military bases in West Germany. An August 1985 bombing at Rhein-Main Air Base near Frankfurt killed two U.S. soldiers and wounded 20 others.

Despite these attacks, the Red Army Faction never succeeded in destabilizing the West German government. And by the late 1980s, Communist states like the Soviet Union and East Germany had entered a period of decline. In November 1989 the Berlin Wall came down, and in October 1990 East and West Germany were reunified under a democratic government. By December 1991 the Soviet Union itself had ceased to exist. As the influence of Communist states eroded, so did the power of left-wing groups.

Still, the Red Army Faction continued to conduct operations through the early 1990s. In February 1991, the RAF assassinated a government official who was overseeing the transfer of state assets from the former East Germany to the new Federal Republic of Germany. In 1993 the RAF detonated explosives at the site of a prison being constructed in Weiterstadt.

Three months after that attack, German GSG 9 agents cornered RAF terrorists Wolfgang Grams and Birgit Hogefeld. A shootout began, and Grams and a German agent were killed. Hogefeld was arrested, and later convicted of several murders related to her terrorist activities with RAF.

Around this time, the Red Army Faction agreed to stop its violence in exchange for the release from prison of some RAF members. The truce remained in place for several years. In April 1998, the group sent a letter to the international news agency Reuters, declaring that it would no longer exist.

During the three decades it was active, the Red Army Faction was responsible for 34 deaths and hundreds of injuries.

RAMZI YOUSEF
BOMBING MASTERMIND

Until 1993, the United States seemed immune to the sort of terrorist attacks that had plagued other countries around the world. During the 1980s and early 1990s Americans had been targeted for attack by Islamic fundamentalists in the Middle East and Europe. However, although these attacks angered Americans, they did not make most people fear for their safety because they had happened far away, on foreign soil. Attitudes changed on February 26, 1993, when a powerful explosion beneath the World Trade Center, in the heart of New York City, told Americans that international terrorism had reached their homeland.

The terrorist mastermind behind this 1993 attack, Ramzi Yousef, was a 26-year-old citizen of Pakistan who had been born in Kuwait in 1967. Yousef's parents were working in Kuwait at the

time. He lived there until the mid-1980s, when his parents returned to Pakistan. Yousef did not go with them; instead, he went to the United Kingdom to attend college. In 1986 he enrolled at Swansea Institute in Wales, where he studied electrical engineering.

Yousef returned to Pakistan during the summers between college semesters. In the late 1980s, he attended mujahideen training camps along the Pakistan-Afghanistan border. At the time, the *mujahideen* were fighting against the Soviet Union, which had occupied Afghanistan since 1979. At the camps—which were funded in part by a wealthy Saudi Arabian named Osama bin Laden—Yousef learned about firearms and how to make bombs. He was encouraged by his uncle, Khalid Sheikh Mohammed, who although just three years older than Yousef had been fighting with the mujahideen for several

In 1993, the twin towers of the World Trade Center dominated New York City's skyline.

years. By the time he graduated from Swansea Institute in 1990, Yousef had become an expert bomb-maker—thanks in part to the electronics skills he had developed in college.

The conflict in Afghanistan had ended in 1989, but soon Muslim fundamentalists found a new enemy: the United States, which had stationed hundreds of thousands of soldiers in Saudi Arabia during the summer of 1990, and led a coalition that invaded Iraq the next year. U.S. support for the state of Israel also angered Muslims.

In 1991, Yousef began planning a terrorist attack in the United States. He decided to detonate several bombs simultaneously in New York. One, he hoped, would bring down the tallest buildings in the city, the twin towers of the World Trade Center, which were a symbol of America's financial system. Other bombs would destroy the United Nations building and the Lincoln and Holland tunnels, which connect Manhattan to New Jersey. The plot was inspired by Omar Abd al-Rahman, a blind Muslim religious leader who was associated with Osama bin Laden. Rahman was living in New York City, where he raised money for militant Islamic groups and coordinated terrorist attacks in Egypt and other countries

CASE FILE

Name: Ramzi Yousef
Born: May 20, 1967
Location of Attacks: New York City,
Number of victims: 6 killed, more than 1,000 injured
Captured: February 1995
Justice: Convicted in 1998 of murder and conspiracy to commit murder; currently serving sentence of life imprisonment with no possibility of parole.

allied with the United States. Yousef's uncle Khaled Sheikh Mohammed helped to formulate the plan and provided funds to help Yousef carry out the attack.

Yousef and a Palestinian associate named Ahmed Ajaj flew to the United States in late 1992. Ajaj was detained by authorities, but Yousef was admitted to the country. He spoke with Rahman, then spent some time contacting the blind cleric's followers in New York and New Jersey. Soon, he had a group that included Mahmud Abouhalima, Mohammad Salameh, Nidal

Omar Abdel Rahman

A. Ayyad, Abdul Rahman Yasin, and Eyad Ismoil. They gathered the chemicals and material needed to construct a large bomb.

By this point, the plan had changed—Yousef felt it would be too difficult to detonate the four bombs simultaneously, so he decided to focus on the twin towers. His plan was to detonate the bomb in a parking garage below the north tower. He hoped the large bomb would cause enough damage that the tower would fall over into the south tower, bringing them both down. Yousef later said that he hoped the attack would kill thousands of people.

At around noon on February 26, Yousef and Eyad Ismoil drove a rented Ryder truck containing the 1,500-pound bomb into the garage beneath the World Trade Center. Yousef lit the four fuses that would ignite the bomb, and the conspirators quickly made their way out of the building. At 12:17 P.M., the bomb exploded.

The blast ripped through the first six floors of the north tower, creating a hole nearly 100 feet across. Yet the tower

Investigators work in the bomb-damaged foundation of the World Trade Center.

The FBI released these photographs of suspects in the 1993 World Trade Center bombing. All but Abdul Yasin were eventually arrested, tried, and convicted for their role in the terrorist attack. Today Yasin, who has never been caught, remains on the FBI's Most Wanted Terrorists list.

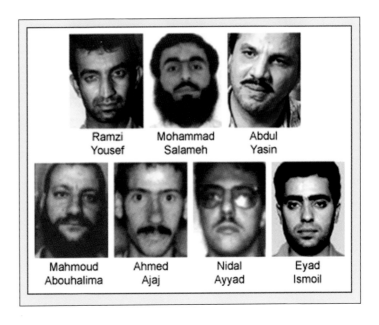

Ramzi Yousef

Mohammad Salameh

Abdul Yasin

Mahmoud Abouhalima

Ahmed Ajaj

Nidal Ayyad

Eyad Ismoil

remained standing. It turned out that Yousef had parked the truck too far from the poured concrete foundation to cause the tower to topple. Also, parts of the bomb failed to detonate. Nonetheless, the towers shook and quickly filled with smoke, and frightened New Yorkers scrambled for the exits. Six people were killed by the blast while more than 1,000 were injured, most as they tried to escape from the damaged building. The bombing caused more than $300 million in damage.

At first investigators thought an electrical transformer had exploded, but from the extend of the damage it was clear a bomb had been detonated. Investigators searched through the rubble for clues, and soon found part of the rental truck. They were able to trace the truck back to the rental agency, and this enabled the FBI to arrest Mohammad Salameh, who had rented the truck for the plotters. Authorities soon rounded up other members of the terrorist network—including the blind cleric Rahman and nine of his followers. However, Yousef escaped being arrested—he had left the country just hours after the World Trade Center bomb exploded, flying to Pakistan where he could hide out with friends and family.

In Pakistan, Yousef was reunited with his uncle, Khaled Sheikh Mohammed, who by this time had become a high-ranking member of Osama bin Laden's al-Qaeda organization. They planned several terrorist attacks, including an attempted assassination of Pakistan's female prime minister, Benazir Bhutto. This attack in the summer of 1993 failed when Yousef's bomb exploded prematurely, injuring his left eye.

The injury didn't stop Yousef from planning and carrying out other attacks. In 1994 he and several others carried out a bombing attack at a Shiite Muslim shrine in Iran. The attack in June 1994 killed 26 Muslims. Yousef also planned bombings at the Israeli and American embassies in Thailand.

In 1994 Osama bin Laden sent Yousef and Khaled Sheikh Mohammed to the Philippines. There, they met with other Islamic radicals. Yousef taught bomb-making courses to would-be terrorists, and they began planning what would have been the biggest terrorist attack in history.

Operation Bojinka involved the bombing of 11 flights originating in Asia.

The first phase of "Operation Bojinka," as Khaled Sheikh Mohammed called the plot, involved planting bombs on 11 passenger airplanes that were flying over the Pacific Ocean to the United States. The bombs would have timers to ensure that they would explode at approximately the same time. The terrorists planned to carry out their plot on January 21, 1995. They expected to kill more than 4,000 people and to paralyze international air traffic.

The ingenious bomb Yousef created used liquid nitroglycerine, which could be smuggled on board an airplane disguised as contact lens cleaning solution. Once on the plane, the bomber could attach the bottle of nitroglycerine to a battery-powered electronic wristwatch, which Yousef had modified to act as a timer and detonator.

On December 11, 1994, Yousef boarded a Boeing 747 jet in Manila that was flying to the Philippine city of Cebu, then on to Tokyo, Japan. This was meant to be a test run. He had the bomb components in his carry-on luggage, and assembled them in the airplane bathroom. He hid the bomb under his seat, and got off the plane when it landed in Cebu. About two hours after Philippine Airlines Flight 434 took off from Cebu, the small bomb exploded, killing a passenger and seriously damaging the aircraft.

The damage could have been much

worse. Yousef had chosen a seat that, in a normal 747 aircraft, was directly over the fuel tank and would have caused the airplane to explode when the bomb went off. However, as luck would have it the seats on Flight 434 had been moved, so the blast did not damage the fuel tank. The plane was able to land safely on a Pacific island. Nonetheless, the bomb had worked perfectly, and Yousef and his associates began preparing additional bombs, which would carry ten times as much explosive, for Operation Bojinka.

On January 7, 1995, Yousef and Abdul Hakim Murad were mixing chemicals to create explosives in an apartment in Manila. When a fire broke out in the kitchen, the two men escaped the apartment. Local firemen came to put out the fire. Yousef had left behind his laptop computer, which contained information about the plot; although he sent Murad to recover it, the terrorist was detained by Filipino police. Yousef fled to Pakistan, while Murad was interrogated by the police. He admitted to being a trained pilot who had been recruited by Yousef for the second phase of Operation Bojinka—to hijack a commercial airplane and fly it into a target in the United States, such as the Pentagon or CIA headquarters. Police also learned that the terrorists had been planning to assassinate Pope John Paul II, head of the Roman Catholic church,

during his scheduled visit to the Philippines in January 1995.

The United States government worked with Pakistan's national police to track down Ramzi Yousef. On February 7, 1995, Pakistani police arrested the terrorist in Islamabad, and turned him over to U.S. authorities the next day. Yousef was flown to the United States to stand trial.

At the airport, police loaded Yousef onto a helicopter, which would take him to the Metropolitan Correctional Center in lower Manhattan. As the craft flew into the city, one of the federal agents lifted Yousef's blindfold so that he could see the still-standing World Trade Center towers. "See, you didn't get them after all," the agent remarked. The handcuffed prisoner fidgeted a moment, then responded, "Not yet."

On September 5, 1996, Yousef, Murad, and another conspirator, Wali Khan Amin Shah, were convicted for their role in the Bojinka plot. All were sentenced to life in prison without parole. On November 12, 1997, Yousef was found guilty of masterminding the 1993 World Trade Center bombing. Since then he has been incarcerated at the federal maximum security prison in Florence, Colorado. It was in a small cell there that on September 11, 2001, he watched as CNN reported on the unfolding terrorist attacks that brought the towers down.

CHAPTER NOTES

p. 9:   "Freedom fighters do not need . . ." Ronald Reagan, "Radio Address to the Nation on Terrorism" (May 31, 1986). The American Presidency Project. http://www.presidency.ucsb.edu/ws/index.php?pid=37376

p. 9:   "the calculated use of unlawful violence . . ." U.S. Department of Defense, "Definition of Terrorism." http://www.defense.gov

p. 9:   "the unlawful use of force . . ." Federal Bureau of Investigation, "What Is Terrorism?" http://www.fbi.gov/stats-services/publications/terrorism-2002-2005

p. 9:   "premeditated politically-motivated violence . . ." quoted in Paul M. Maniscalo, *Homeland Security: Principles and Practice of Terrorism Response* (Sudbury, Mass.: Jones and Bartlett Publishers, 2010), p. 3.

p. 20:   "There is no more important duty . . ." Osama bin Laden, "Declaration of War Against the Americans Occupying the Land of the Two Holy Places." (August 23, 1996). http://www.pbs.org/newshour/updates/military/july-dec96/fatwa_1996.html

p. 20:   "Terrorising you, while you . . ." Ibid.

p. 20:   "To kill the Americans and their allies . . ." Osama bin Laden," Al-Qaeda's Second Fatwa," (February 23, 1998). http://www.pbs.org/newshour/updates/military/jan-june98/fatwa_1998.html

p. 21:   "part of a continuing effort . . ." William S. Cohen, quoted in Douglas J. Gillert, "U.S. Strikes Against Terrorist Forces" American Forces Press Service (August 20, 1998). http://www.defense.gov/News/NewsArticle.aspx?ID=43223

p. 24:   "I want justice . . ." George W. Bush, quoted in "Bush: Bin Laden 'Wanted Dead or Alive'" CNN (September 17, 2001). http://articles.cnn.com/2001-09-17/us/bush.powell.terrorism_1_bin-qaeda-terrorist-attacks?_s=PM:US

p. 38:   "largest non-nuclear blast . . ." quoted in U.S. Department of Defense, *Report of the DOD Commission on Beirut International Airport Terrorist Act*, October 23, 1983 (December 20, 1983), p. 63.

p. 45:   "strategic, historic, and divine victory." Hasan Nasrallah, "victory rally" speech transcript, *The Muslim Observer* (September 26, 2006). http://muslimmedianetwork.com/mmn/?p=384

p. 51:   "Irish republicans have continued . . . " Susanne Breen, "Former Provos claim Kerr murder and vow more attacks" *Belfast Telegraph* (April 22, 2011). http://www.belfasttelegraph.co.uk/news/local-national/northern-ireland/former-provos-claim-kerr-murder-and-vow-more-attacks-15146426.html#ixzz2Ey73KmcZ

p. 55:   "We blew up Thomas Mosser . . ." Unabomber letter published as "Bombing in Sacramento: The Letter, Excerpts from Letter by 'Terrorist Group' FC, Which Says it Sent Bombs," *New York Times* (April 26, 1995). http://www.nytimes.com/1995/04/26/us/bombing-sacramento-letter-excerpts-letter-terrorist-group-fc-which-says-it-sent.html?scp=3&sq=Thomas+Mosser&st=nyt&gwh=2E62A511E588ECEE8C7337BFCE2FBACC

p. 62:   "Foremost, the bombing . . ." Timothy McVeigh, quoted in Gore Vidal, "The Meaning of Timothy McVeigh," *Vanity Fair* (September 2001). http://www.vanityfair.com/politics/features/2001/09/mcveigh200109

p. 62:   "shook the daylights . . ." Sue Anne Pressley, "Bomb Kills Dozens in Oklahoma Federal Building," *Washington Post* (April 20, 1995), p. A1.

p. 68:   "Armed struggle is the only way . . ." The Palestinian National Charter (July 17, 1968). http://www.mfa.gov.il/MFA/Peace+Process/Guide+to+the+Peace+Process/The+Palestinian+National+Charter.htm

p. 87:   "See, you didn't get . . ." Peter Lance, *100 Years for Revenge: International Terrorism and the FBI* (New York: HarperCollins, 2003), p. 298.

p. 87:   "Not yet." Ibid.

GLOSSARY

al-Qaeda—an international Islamist terror organization established in Afghanistan in 1989; led by Osama bin Laden, it orchestrated the attacks of September 11, 2001, as well as many others against U.S. and other targets.

aphorism—a short, truthful statement that is cleverly written.

biological weapon—a microorganism (bacteria) that can be spread by terrorists to cause illness or death.

caliphate—an Islamic state ruled by a Muslim spiritual and temporal leader.

infidel—a person who does not believe in Islam.

jihad—holy war. Some Muslims interpret *jihad* as a requirement to fight non-Muslims, while others see it as a personal struggle for spiritual discipline.

mujahideen—Islamic holy warriors, or warriors involved in a holy war (*jihad*).

nerve agent—a chemical substance, such as sarin, that interferes with the central nervous system and can cause incapacitation or death.

secular—non-religious.

Sharia—a code of Islamic law, based on the Qur'an as well as the example of the Prophet Muhammad and his earliest Muslim followers.

Shia—the second-largest branch of Islam, which claims about 15 percent of the religion's followers worldwide and which rejects the legitimacy of all Muslim caliphs not directly descended from the prophet Muhammad through the line of Ali. Shiites are a majority in Lebanon and Iran.

Sunni—Islam's dominant branch, with about 80 percent of all believers.

theocracy—a government whose officials claim to be divinely guided.

umma—the worldwide community of Muslims.

FURTHER READING

Bergen, Peter L. *Manhunt: The Ten-Year Search for Bin Laden from 9/11 to Abbottabad*. New York: Crown Publishing, 2012.

Blanford, Nicholas. *Warriors of God: Inside Hezbollah's Thirty-Year Struggle Against Israel*. New York: Random House, 2011.

Chase, Alston. *Harvard and the Unabomber: The Education of an American Terrorist*. New York: W.W. Norton and Company, 2003.

Combs, Cynthia C. *Terrorism in the Twenty-First Century*. 7th ed. Upper Saddle River, N.J.: Pearson, 2012.

Habeck, Mary. *Knowing the Enemy: Jihadist Ideology and the War on Terror*. New Haven: Yale University Press, 2007.

Lance, Peter. *100 Years for Revenge: International Terrorism and the FBI*. New York: HarperCollins, 2003.

McDermott, Terry, and Josh Meyer. *The Hunt for KSM: Inside the Pursuit and Takedown of the real 9/11 Mastermind, Khalid Sheikh Mohammed*. Boston: Little, Brown and Co., 2012.

Maniscalo, Paul M. *Homeland Security: Principles and Practice of Terrorism Response*. Sudbury, Mass.: Jones and Bartlett Publishers, 2010.

Michel, Lou, and Dan Herbeck. *American Terrorist: Timothy McVeigh and the Oklahoma City Bombing*. New York: HarperCollins, 2001.

Mobley, Blake W. *Terrorism and Counterintelligence: How Terrorist Groups Elude Detection*. New York: Colombia University Press, 2012.

Post, Jerrold M. *The Mind of the Terrorist: The Psychology of Terrorism from the IRA to al-Qaeda*. New York: Palgrave MacMillan, 2007.

INTERNET RESOURCES

http://www.terrorismanswers.org

This site, maintained by the Council on Foreign Relations, tackles the most recent issues concerning terrorist groups. It also profiles individual groups and their beliefs.

http://www.ict.org.il

The home page of the International Policy Institute for Counter-Terrorism offers articles, news, and analysis of the worldwide fight against terrorism.

http://www.state.gov/j/ct

Website of the U.S. State Department's Bureau of Counterterrorism, which includes links to annual reports on global terrorism and the official government list of foreign terrorist organizations.

http://www.9-11commission.gov

The official 2004 report of the National Commission on Terrorist Attacks Upon the United States (also known as the 9/11 Commission) about the September 11, 2001, al-Qaeda attack on the United States is available for download from this government site.

http://www.fbi.gov/about-us/investigate/terrorism

This official FBI website provides information about the agency's work combating terrorism, including analysis, intelligence reports, and links to information about major cases.

INDEX

Numbers in ***bold italics*** refer to captions.

About the Author: Dorothy Kavanaugh is a freelance writer who lives near Philadelphia. She holds a bachelors' degree in elementary education from Bryn Mawr College. She has written numerous books for young adults, including *Islam, Christianity, and Judaism* (2004), *Islam in Asia: Facts and Figures* (2009), and *Sudan and Southern Sudan* (2013).